Construction cost appraisal

Construction cost appraisal

DCF TECHNIQUES

IN THE

CONSTRUCTION INDUSTRY

COLIN DENT MPhil, FRICS

Distributed Exclusively By

INTERNATIONAL IDEAS INC.
1627 Spruce Street
Philadelphia PA USA 19103

First published in Great Britain by
George Godwin Limited, 1974

© Colin Dent 1974

ISBN 0 7114 3308 9

George Godwin Limited
The book publishing subsidiary
of The Builder Group
2–4 Catherine Street
London WC2

Printed and bound in Great Britain by
Eyre & Spottiswoode Ltd
Thanet Press, Union Crescent, Margate

Contents

i

Text figures

Worked examples

Abbreviations used in the text

ACC	annual capital charge
AE	annual equivalent
APF	amount of pound factor
APPF	amount of pound per annum factor
ASF	annual sinking fund
AV	annual value
BCIS	Building Cost Information Service
BMCIS	Building Maintenance Cost Information Service
CFA	Cash Flow Analysis (computer program)
DCF	discounted cash flow
IA	initial allowance
IBM	International Business Machines United Kingdom Ltd
ICL	International Computers Ltd
IQS	Institute of Quantity Surveyors
IRR	internal rate of return
K	thousand
NPV	net present value
PACIN	Program for Analysis of Capital INvestment
PROP	Profit Rating of Projects (computer program)
PROSPER	PROfit Simulation, Planning and Evaluation of Risk (computer program)
PV	present value
PVF	present value factor
RICS	Royal Institution of Chartered Surveyors
SF	sinking fund
TV	terminal value
WDA	writing down allowance
WDV	written down value
YP	years purchase
YPF	years purchase factor

Preface

In recent years the examination requirements of students entering the surveying and building management professions have increasingly called for a knowledge of DCF (ie, discounted cash flow) techniques, often under the various guises of 'cost-in-use studies', 'investment appraisal techniques', 'feasibility studies' and the like. At the same time, the practising surveyor and building developer are becoming aware of the need to use the cash flow techniques now available to management accountants. The aim of this book is therefore two-fold: firstly to cover existing examination requirements of bodies such as the RICS and IQS, and secondly to deal with the incidence of taxation, and the more advanced methods of yield analysis (including computer systems) in an attempt to make the book (*a*) of more practical value to surveyors, building economists and developers, and (*b*) suitable as a textbook for students taking degrees or post-graduate diplomas in building economics, construction management, town planning, etc.

Broadly speaking, the first half of the book is intended to cover existing professional examination requirements in this field, and in this connection I am grateful to both the Royal Institution of Chartered Surveyors and the Institute of Quantity Surveyors for kind permission to reproduce questions set in past examination papers. I must hasten to add that the answers to these questions in this book were supplied entirely by the author, however, who is alone responsible for the accuracy or otherwise of these. Needless to say, they are intended as examples to illustrate basic principles rather than as model answers. In reproducing the questions themselves, the liberty has been taken, in the interests of conformity, of converting the data to metric and, where appropriate, to decimal currency also, in the case of questions set before this became the practice.

The concluding chapters deal with more advanced aspects of the subject, and here I should like to acknowledge the kindness of George Etherington, Senior Lecturer in Accountancy and Taxation at Southampton College of Technology for reading the typescript of the chapter on Company Taxation; and also David Hembury, Senior Lecturer in Construction Management at the same college, who read the section of typescript describing his CFA computer method.

Also my thanks are due to IBM United Kingdom Ltd for their kind permission to describe the PACIN system and reproduce a sample printout; to International Computers Ltd for permission to publish copyright material in connection with both the PROP and the PROSPER computer systems; and to the RICS for allowing me to include a list of elements and some definitions from the Building Maintenance Cost Information Service and the Standard Form of Cost Analysis. Finally, I should like to acknowledge the work of John Carling, who programmed the computer which produced the discount tables at the end of this book.

Southampton **Colin Dent**

Chapter 1
Cost planning and appraisal

Any project involving the outlay of a substantial sum of money requires prudent thought beforehand to ensure that the money is being wisely spent if invested in the project. To assist in reaching a correct decision as to the viability of the project concerned, it will be desirable to quantify the problem in some way, and this will be especially necessary in the case of complex projects (such as building schemes for instance) which involve a series of outlays spread over a period of time, and possibly a series of income payments as well.

To do this it will first be necessary to estimate as accurately as possible the various sums of money involved, and as precisely as possible the times at which they will be either paid or received: to assemble the data in fact. This data will then need to be manipulated in such a way as to provide a basis for answering the question of whether the money is being wisely spent or not. But there are other questions which will probably follow before the decision to go ahead with the project can be confidently taken—such as, would the money be even more wisely spent on an alternative project? Or could the present project be adapted so as to increase its ultimate profitability, or to reduce its initial outlay while retaining its present viability? Or perhaps it would be better simply to leave the money where it is, in the bank, to earn interest or to pay off the overdraft; or to plough it back into the firm?

Techniques for manipulating data so as to provide a numerical basis for answering questions about the financial viability of capital projects have been in use for some time. According to E. J. Broster, discounting techniques were practised by accountants for assessing the financial results of investment projects as long ago as 1930. In recent years, however, these techniques have been refined and brought into wider use by management accountants and others using a concept which has come to be known as discounted cash flow (DCF), and which now forms the basis of the majority of project assessment systems.

Project appraisal terminology

The assessment of a project in order to determine its probable financial soundness will, as we have seen, involve collecting data and then manipulating it in a suitable way. If we wanted to assess the viability of an existing or past project, we could collect factual data of course. But since we shall normally wish to assess the project before committing any money to it, the data will need to be in the form of estimated figures, subsequently to be processed mathematically. Hence the assessment is partly an estimate, and partly a numerical analysis. The word *appraisal* has been used by J. Southwell and others in this connection, especially when applying such assessments to building and civil engineering construction projects, and this has given rise to variations such as *cost appraisal* and *investment appraisal*. Other terms in use are *investment analysis, project analysis*, and, in a slightly narrower sense, *DCF analysis, yield analysis*, etc.

When applied to building projects, the term 'cost appraisal' has the merit of official blessing by the Royal Institution of Chartered Surveyors, in the title of one of its published reports,* although a project assessment may, and usually does, take the benefits (eg, income) into consideration as well as the costs. Then again, past RICS and IQS examination papers have used the term *feasibility study* to describe a cost appraisal at the feasibility stage of a project. On the other hand, a *cost benefit analysis* (CBA) is something else again, referring to a project assessment where benefits (or costs for that matter) other than monetary are to be somehow quantified and taken into account in the calculations. CBA is thus a form of cost appraisal used to assess public works at the planning stage, and is also based on the use of DCF techniques.

It might be worth pointing out that the term 'cost analysis' should not be used when referring to a project assessment, since this term has been pre-empted by the cost planner to mean the elemental analysis of a bill of quantities (as in, for example, 'standard form of cost analysis'). The Institution of Civil Engineers uses the term 'project appraisal' when referring to financial assessment in its publication *An Introduction to Civil Engineering Economics*.

This present book deals with the initial, annual and periodic costs of construction projects, as well as with the cost of taxation. Income may be taken into consideration in some instances in order to compare profitability, set cost limits, or assess taxation; but even in these cases, it is costs rather than revenue which are being analysed. The techniques of appraising such costs apply equally to building and civil engineering projects; any type of construction project in fact. Therefore the term *construction cost appraisal* is probably the most appropriate for use in the present context, and forms the title of this book.

Cost planning

The cost appraisal of construction projects might be carried out by account-ants, engineers, valuers, economists or quantity surveyors, acting on behalf of private or public developers, who themselves must take the final decision, based on conclusions drawn from the cost appraisal. The quantity surveyor is especially well equipped to provide the estimates of initial costs in such cases, since he is a professional cost consultant by training and experience.

*Total Building Cost Appraisal, RICS, 1967.

He may also be defined as a specialised technical accountant (he adjusts the final accounts of construction projects in fact) and would therefore appear equally qualified to perform the numerical manipulations of the data and the interpretation of results.

Traditional quantity surveying services however cast the surveyor in the role of technical cost accountant rather than management accountant, and consequently the traditional quantity surveyor does not think naturally in terms of rates of interest and yield percentages, corporation tax and investment incentives, sinking-funds and loan redemption; at least, not when performing his function as contract quantity surveyor. But such matters are the stock-in-trade of management accountancy and necessary concepts in project appraisal work. The traditional role of the quantity surveyor has broadened out in recent years however, notably into the field of building economics and cost planning, which was first introduced into the RICS examination syllabus in 1961. This new syllabus—covering such aspects as private and public investment; capital, maintenance and running costs; anticipated return and developer's budget—placed the quantity surveyor in a better position technically to give something of a cost appraisal service to the client. But it did more than this. It also covered the full range of cost planning disciplines and techniques, turning the quantity surveyor into a qualified cost planner. Nineteen sixty-one was also the year in which the Building Cost Information Service (BCIS) was established by the RICS to provide a continual backing of technical, financial and statistical data in support of the cost planning services of its members. And the launching of the new Standard Form of Cost Analysis in 1970, prepared jointly on behalf of the BCIS and the (then) Ministry of Public Building and Works, which laid down an agreed basic format for cost plan preparation on a national basis, marked the establishment of cost planning as a major service provided by the quantity surveying profession.

Now cost planning may be thought of as a system for monitoring costs at *design* stage so that (*a*) the tender does not exceed the preliminary estimate, and (*b*) the costs are deployed in such a way as to give the best value for money. But if cost planning is to be of maximum value to the client, it should clearly not be confined to the design stage of projects, but should be extended forward into the construction stage by means of budgetary control systems, and backwards into the early feasibility and planning stages as well, so that financial control may be fully effective in providing value for money at all stages, and so that decisions taken or circumstances occurring before or after design stage do not tend to invalidate the whole object of the exercise. Hence the quantity-surveyor-turned-cost-planner needs to be fully in the financial picture at the inception stage of a project in order to give his best service. For cost planning in any real sense starts with a cost appraisal of the project in order to establish its overall *cost limit*, ie, the total budget used at cost plan preparation stage for the purpose of fixing *cost targets* (totals for the cost analysis *elements* into which the project is sub-divided). Cost appraisal may therefore legitimately be regarded as a branch of cost planning, and one which the quantity surveyor will be increasingly expected to provide as part of his overall cost planning service.

Costs-in-use

There is also another reason why cost appraisal must be a tool of the cost planner, and this is to do with design-stage cost planning. At this stage it is necessary to carry out a series of *cost checks* to monitor the actual design process from the cost plan. In essence, each element of the design is costed, and if necessary re-designed and re-costed as the design progresses. With some systems (known as *comparative* rather than *elemental* systems) alternative design solutions to individual elements are costed and presented as choices to the designer.

Now it will be obvious that the costing of elements may be misleading if initial cost only is considered for, as P. A. Stone points out,* the cost of construction is only the first cost incurred for a building. Over its life it needs to be maintained and serviced. And he goes on to show that if the construction cost is spread over the life of a building in the form of a mortgage payment, the annual amount may be no more than equivalent to the average annual costs of maintenance and servicing; citing an example of estimates for a light factory building which gave the equivalent annual cost of only about 50 per cent of the total equivalent annual costs, including maintenance and running costs. This situation may be modified as a result of taxation allowances of course.

In short, the ultimate best buy may not be the cheapest article, so the cost planner needs to be aware of both the first cost and the ultimate cost of the design solutions offered, if he is to carry out his task of planning the best buy. More than this: he needs to be able to back his awareness by facts and figures, for which he needs to employ the techniques of cost appraisal.

The term *costs-in-use*† is employed in the RICS syllabus in this connection to denote the total costs (initial and subsequent costs) which are reduced to a common denominator for the purpose of appraising the true (ultimate) costs of a design element in comparison with other design solutions, similarly reduced. This process will be fully explained in later chapters, but at this juncture it will be sufficient to make the point that cost-in-use studies at design stage of a project are cost appraisals which use the same concepts and techniques as those referred to earlier—DCF techniques in fact, borrowed from the realms of management accountancy, but applied to individual parts of a project at detailed design stage, instead of (or as well as) to the entire project at feasibility stage.

---

*Building Economy, Design, Production and Organisation, Pergamon Press, 1966.

†The hyphenated form used here is that recommended by Dent & Southwell, in 'Quantity Surveying Terminology', *The Chartered Surveyor*, August, 1966.

Building economics

The study and use of cost appraisal techniques, and their adaptation to cost planning and cost consultancy problems by quantity surveyors is in line with the expanding scope of the quantity surveying profession into the broader field of building economics in recent years. This has been brought about by a number of factors: demand for cost planning services and cost consultancy, increased complexity of projects, use of processing systems for contract documentation, increase in full-time professional education, and increased economic inflation and higher interest rates demanding more sophisticated cost control. Whatever the reasons, there is no doubt that the role of the quantity surveyor today is becoming more that of a specialised economist giving service to the construction industry over a wider field of disciplines than that of simply preparing a bill of quantities. Cost appraisal techniques and the use of DCF analysis are essential subjects for study by the building economist, especially since these subjects are themselves often thought of as a branch of applied economics.

Real estate valuation

Mention has been made above of valuers, and it will be appropriate here to comment briefly on the functions of the valuer in relation to the building economist as a practitioner of cost appraisal, for their methods of approach are often thought to be somewhat similar. For instance, building economists frequently use valuation tables for cost appraisal purposes, and this fact alone might tend to suggest that a valuation and a cost appraisal are really one and the same thing. Added colour is lent to this view by the inclusion of *factors affecting land values* in the RICS building economics syllabus, which has led to the appearance of 'methods of valuation' in the teaching curricula of quantity surveying courses. Does this perhaps mean that the building economist is usurping the province of the valuer?

Such is not the case, for a cost appraisal is only superficially similar to a valuation, its basic purpose being dissimilar, and its whole approach different in consequence. The basic purpose of a valuation is to establish the *market* value of a property, ie, its resale value on the open market. The only way to establish this with absolute certainty is of course to actually sell the property; but a notional market value can be obtained by methods of valuation, which attempt to assess the amount which could theoretically be obtained if the property were put on the market and offered to a purchaser able and willing to buy. Now the first and obvious method of valuation is to observe the price being fetched by similar properties in the same area and to assess the value accordingly. In the case of commercial and industrial property, or investment or leasehold property it may not be quite so easy as this however, and calculations of the monetary worth of the property to a prospective purchaser, based on the rents obtainable from it (notional or otherwise) will need to be made in order to help establish a notional resale value. Valuations for most purposes are based on this general principle, whether for rating assessment, compulsory purchase, commercial acquisition, leasehold transaction or owner occupation.

A cost appraisal, on the other hand, is basically an assessment not of the market value to a purchaser, but of the financial value to a developer. Although rents (if any) may be taken into consideration, this will not be in order (at least not primarily) to establish a market value to a notional purchaser, but to establish the degree of financial viability to the owner. Of course, the theoretical market value may be a factor to be taken into consideration; but it will be apparent that a building scheme (say a factory building) might be a very profitable project from the point of view of a manufacturer who happens to need a new factory of a certan kind on a certain site, whereas the price which that particular factory might fetch if placed on the open market might be quite uneconomic if there happened to be no other manufacturer in the area with a need for such a building. Hence the general aims of a valuation and a cost appraisal differ, and so must the general approach and detailed calculations.

In this connexion it is interesting to observe that the ninth edition of *Parry's Valuation Tables** (renamed *Parry's Valuation Tables and Conversion Tables*) contains for the first time a set of discounted cash flow tables, and makes the comment that such tables are frequently used by accountants for financial analysis of proposed projects, and indicates that they are also used by economists.

It may perhaps be asked why, if a cost appraisal differs from a valuation, should 'methods of valuation' be included in a building economics curriculum at all? The answer firstly—as indicated above—is that the ultimate market value of the project may be a factor to be taken into consideration when a cost appraisal is being undertaken. Secondly, and perhaps more importantly, the acquisition of the site will usually need to be included in the calculations, and its value may need to be established before purchase. Thirdly, a question of apportionment of value may be required at some stage in the appraisal. Should any or all of these circumstances arise, it is not to be inferred that the QS/building economist should turn himself into a valuation surveyor and practise methods of valuation; only that he needs to know enough about such methods to know when to recommend calling in the expert, and how to recognise a situation in which an actual valuation may be necessary. In the same way the valuer, as a general practice surveyor, needs to know enough about measurement and contract procedure to know when to call on the services of the quantity surveyor.

Use of discount tables

Although valuation tables may be used for cost appraisal purposes, this is due to the somewhat fortuitous fact that they happen to represent the same mathematical concepts as those which underlie DCF analysis, rather than

Estates Gazette, 1969.

because of a close affinity of purpose with valuation techniques. Accountants, investment analysts and financial economists usually use ordinary discount tables instead. But being surveyors, building economists tend to use the tables of their colleagues the valuation surveyors, which are really discount tables specially prepared for valuers. Why then, it may be asked, do they include special DCF tables if the valuation tables themselves are suitable for cost appraisal purposes? Only because of their convenience of format for certain operations, though for most appraisal exercises it may well be found convenient to ignore the DCF tables and use the valuation tables themselves.*

The use by building economists of valuation tables for the purpose of cost appraisal is exemplified in the terminology employed by the RICS in its examination papers in Building Economics and Cost Planning, where, for example, *years purchase (single rate)* has been used more than once when referring to a table giving the present value of an annuity. In accordance with this custom, and to avoid confusing students of building economics, valuation-table terminology will be used where appropriate in this book. At the same time it will be appreciated that neither valuation, discount, or any other form of tables are absolutely necessary in cost appraisal work, since they are merely a device for reducing the mathematical work involved by enabling us to look up a factor instead of working it out by means of a fairly simple formula. It is in any case desirable for us to understand the formulae represented by the tables, so that we can use them if we have to, and so that we can better comprehend the numerical and financial concepts implied by the tables which they represent.

These concepts will be examined in detail in the chapters which follow.

---

*A set of tables suitable for most discounting purposes will be found at the end of this book.

Chapter 2
The PV method of comparison

There may be such things as absolute values in philosophy or religion, but in economics values are relative. An article is worth £x because you consider it worthwhile to forego spending the £x on something else, assuming your money supply to be finite and your ultimate demands insatiable—a classic economic axiom based on a common human frailty. The assessment of economic growth is therefore a matter of comparison, and one way of comparing projects is to compare their initial costs. The housewife does this all the time when shopping in the supermarket, on her 'project' to buy consumer goods. But in the case of consumer durables, there are running costs and replacement costs to take into consideration as well, so that the cheapest article which will do the job satisfactorily to start with will not necessarily be the best buy in the end. One of the most expensive consumer durables of all is real estate, and because the amount of money required for property development is relatively great, it will be essential to take the running and replacement costs into account when comparing alternative projects. But these are future costs as opposed to present-day initial costs of buying the land and erecting the building, and we cannot simply add the future to the present costs to give us a grand total, because we shall not be adding like to like, for the following reasons.

The concept of discounting
Consider the statement: a pound today is worth more than a pound tomorrow, today.

Now we might also say: a pound today is worth more than a pound tomorrow, tomorrow. This is because a pound will actually be worth less than a pound when tomorrow comes, due to inflation. But even if we ignore inflation altogether, the pound we receive tomorrow is worth less to us today than the pound we receive today because, had we in fact received it today, we could have put it in the bank and by tomorrow it would have earned one day's interest. But we could not do this because we did not have it today, and it will be worth less by the amount of interest when we finally get it tomorrow.

Interest is not of course calculated daily in the ordinary way, but the general principle holds good, which is simply that money in the bank earns compound interest over a period of time, and money invested is presumed to grow at a compound interest rate. The actual interest rate is a measure of the degree of risk involved in the investment, and because the risk of the bank collapsing is very small, the interest we get from a deposit account is likewise small. It should not be forgotten however that the money put in the bank may be reducing an overdraft at 10 per cent rather than earning interest at $2\frac{1}{2}$ per cent, which is equivalent to earning interest at 10 per cent. However this may be, and however small the interest rate, the fact remains that, provided the money is invested wisely and not rashly, it will earn *some* interest—the presumption being of course that the money belongs to that gentleman of legal fiction, an ordinary prudent man.

Given the fact that all money is presumed invested at compound interest, then it becomes worth more tomorrow provided we can lay our hands on it today and consequently invest it (ignoring inflation effect, which will be dealt with separately later). Now it follows from this that the sooner we receive the money, the more interest it will have accumulated by a given date in the future; while money received (and invested) later will have accumulated less interest by that future date. Therefore we can compare the *ultimate* value of sums paid out (or received) at different times in the future by merely selecting a date after which they will all have been paid, and calculating the amount of interest they will each have earned by then. The sums paid in last will earn least interest, but larger sums will earn more interest than smaller ones, so we shall have found a means of accounting for both the *amount* of payment and the *time* of payment. The value so arrived at is known as the terminal value (TV) of the sums of money (principal and interest); and when all such values in a given project are added together, the sum is known as the TV of the project.

The formula for finding the terminal value of one pound after n years is:

$$TV = (1 + r)^n$$

where r is the rate of interest; and this is the ordinary compound interest formula where the principal (the sum deposited) is made equal to one pound so that the result is a factor by which any sum may be multiplied to give its terminal value.

Thus the TV of £100 in 3 years at 10 per cent would be:

$$TV = (1 + r)^n$$
$$= (1 + 0 \cdot 10)^3$$
$$= (1 \cdot 10)^3$$
$$= 1 \cdot 331$$
$$\text{hence TV of £100} = 100 \times 1 \cdot 331$$
$$= £133 \cdot 10$$

Notice that r is expressed as a rate per cent, ie, as a decimal fraction after division by one hundred.

We have seen how, at an interest rate of 10 per cent, £100 increases its value in 3 years to £133·10; and it will be obvious that we could select year n to represent the conclusion of a project, and by compounding all sums expended during the project in this way, we should have allowed for the fact of their occurrence at different points along the time-scale by allowing for the

differential amounts of interest involved. They can then be added together
to obtain the terminal value of the project, against which the terminal value
of other projects can be directly measured to give a cost comparison.

In practice however it will usually be more convenient to do just the
opposite and, instead of finding the terminal value, to find the *present* value.
There are two main reasons for this: (*a*) because schemes of differing lengths
of life will have differing terminal years, invalidating comparison of terminal
values, and (*b*) because reduction of future sums to present-day values which
can be directly related to today's construction costs tends to make com-
parisons more meaningful. As might be expected, the formula for finding the
present value of a future sum is the reciprocal of that for finding the future
value of a present sum, viz:

$$PV = \frac{1}{(1 + r)^n}$$

and the process involved is known as *discounting*.

This last word is usually thought to mean the making of a 'deduction from
amount due or price of goods in consideration of its being paid promptly
or in advance' (to quote the *Concise Oxford Dictionary*) and surveyors are
well accustomed to this usage as a result of dealing with the accounts of
nominated sub-contractors and suppliers. But the dictionary gives an alternative meaning of discount as being to lessen or detract from; and its use in
this sense to mean the reciprocal of compounding is well established.

To avoid unnecessary arithmetic, tables are usually consulted when
compounding or discounting. The table of compound interest, giving the
amount to which £1 will increase in n years at a given rate of interest is called
the *amount of pound* table in the valuation tables previously referred to. The
factor obtained from this table is therefore referred to as the amount of
pound factor (APF). Similarly, the factor obtained from the tables giving the
present value of one pound will be referred to as the present value factor
(PVF).

Thus, if C_0 represents the initial cost of a project, and C_p a cost occurring
at some future period, we may express the present value of the project by
means of the following table-directive equation:

$$PV = C_0 + \Sigma(PVF \times C_p)$$

It might be wise to make clear at this point that the above PVF refers to the
table *with no allowance for the effect of income tax on interest accumulations*.
The incidence of taxation is dealt with separately in later chapters.

Cash flow

We have seen that sums of money payable in the future may be discounted
to their present value which, when summated and added to the present-day
cost of the project, will represent the present value of the project as a whole.
The present value of any such sum is a product of its magnitude and its point

on the time-scale. The present value of £100 in 3 years time discounted at 10 per cent is:

$$100 \times 0.75(PVF) = £75$$

But in 20 years time £100 is reduced to:

$$100 \times 0.15(PVF) = \text{a mere £15 present value} .$$

The present value of a sum depends on the exact time at which it is actually received or paid, not the time at which it may be theoretically due.

The aims and purposes of company accounts are, broadly speaking, to obtain a periodic balance sheet showing the overall position of the company at the end of the period. But any accounting process which employs the principle of discounting in order to arrive at its financial conclusions must ensure that its entries are only in respect of the actual transference of cash, since the timing of each cash transfer will directly affect its ultimate numerical value. Systems of accounting which rely on this principle are called cash flow systems. They are used to calculate profit yield over a period, rather than for balance-sheet purposes, for which double-entry book-keeping systems of the conventional kind are employed. Cash flow systems which do not employ discounting have been used in the past (eg, payback systems, rate of return on capital, ACC using interest on half-capital, etc) but nowadays cash flow systems for assessing profitability usually employ discounting methods as these generally give more accurate results. They are all based on the concept of calculating the present value of future cash flows by means of discounting.

Initial and periodic costs
As a simple example of the use of the PV method of comparison involving initial costs followed by periodic maintenance costs, let us consider the following question.

EXAMPLE 1

Problem

You have been asked to advise on which of the following three alternatives for windows is the most economic from the combined viewpoint of capital costs and maintenance costs.

a Softwood windows costing initially £600 fixed complete and requiring to be repainted every fifth year at a cost of £50.

b Hardwood windows costing initially £800 fixed complete and requiring to be treated every tenth year at a cost of £20.

c Anodized aluminium windows at a cost of £1400 fixed complete and not requiring any significant periodic maintenance.

For the purpose of this question you are to assume that the life of the building will be 40 years and that the compound interest rate will be 5 per cent, and to ignore current tax regulations regarding maintenance costs.

Show the calculations you would make before giving your advice. The table given below shows the amount which must be invested now (ignoring tax) in order to accumulate to £1 at 5 per cent compound interest over a given number of years.

Years	PV factor
5	0·784
10	0·614
15	0·481
20	0·377
25	0·295
30	0·231
35	0·181

Solution

a Softwood windows   £
Initial cost   600

Periodic costs: £50 every 5 years:

5 yrs	= 0·784
10	= 0·614
15	= 0·481
20	= 0·377
25	= 0·295
30	= 0·231
35	= 0·181

PV = 2·963 × 50   148

Present value of softwood windows   £748

b Hardwood windows   £
Initial cost   800

Periodic costs: £20 every 10 years:

$$10 \text{ yrs} = 0 \cdot 614$$
$$20 \quad = 0 \cdot 377$$
$$30 \quad = 0 \cdot 231$$

$$\overline{}$$

$$PV = 1 \cdot 222 \times 20 \qquad 24$$

$$\overline{}$$

Present value of hardwood windows   £824

	£
c Aluminium windows	
Initial cost	1400
Periodic costs: nil	—
	———
Present value of aluminium windows	£1400

Therefore the softwood windows are most economic from the combined viewpoint of capital costs and maintenance costs.

Note 1. It will be observed that the formula:
$$PV = C_0 + \Sigma(PVF \times C_p)$$
has been modified slightly for the purpose of the above example to:
$$PV = C_0 = \Sigma PVF(C_p) \ .$$
This is because the periodic costs happen to be constant in both instances, making it possible and logical to short-circuit the arithmetic by summating the PV factors instead of itemising each PVF by its cost separately.

Note 2. The life of the building is given in the question as 40 years. It has been assumed in the solution that expenditure on periodic maintenance is not required in year 40, since this is the year in which the building is demolished. In the case of leasehold property however, a full repairing lease may well require any such periodic payments to be allowed for in the final year, prior to handing over the building at expiration of the lease.

Annual costs

Costs can be divided into three main kinds, namely:
    (1) initial (eg, building and site costs)
    (2) periodic (eg, maintenance costs of repainting etc)
    (3) annual (eg, running costs of heating etc).

    Annual costs, ie, costs involving a constant annual sum, could be dealt with in the same way as periodic costs; each annual sum could be discounted to its present value by means of the PV table. But if we wished to find the present value of an annual sum over the life of a 40 year project, we should then need to make 40 separate calculations, or at least 40 different table references. What is needed is a formula for finding the present value not of one pound, but of one pound per annum.

If we put one pound in the bank each year for a number of years, we obtain compound interest on a principal which is steadily increasing, the formula for calculating the terminal value of which is:

$$\text{APPF} = \frac{(1 + r)^n - 1}{r}$$

The compound interest table (amount of pound table) gives us the APF with which to multiply the principal in order to obtain its terminal value. The table giving us the terminal value of s series of principals, or *annuity*, is called the *amount of pound per annum* table, giving us the amount of pound per annum factor (APPF), as above.

Now the present value (as opposed to the terminal value) of an annuity is given by the formula:

$$\text{YPF} = \frac{1 - (1 + r)^{-n}}{r}$$

which is not quite a straight-forward reciprocal of the amount of pound per annum table, as one might perhaps suppose it would be. The reciprocal is one of time rather than of algebraic concept.

In the above equation YPF stands for years purchase factor, derived from the term *years purchase*, a rather quaint valuer's term given as the title of the valuation tables representing the present value of one pound per annum.

Dual rate years purchase
When using valuation tables it is all too easy to look up dual rate years purchase in mistake for single rate years purchase, and the student should be guarded against making this mistake. A brief explanation of the difference between the two sets of tables might be appropriate here.

It will be seen that the formula for years purchase, ie, present value of one pound per annum, viz:

$$\frac{1 - (1 + r)^{-n}}{r}$$

contains r twice. Now r is the rate of interest, and if we are using this formula to simulate the time-reciprocal of the terminal value of one pound per annum at compound interest, the innate presumption is that the interest is left in to grow, not taken out and re-invested during the term at a different interest rate. Hence each r has the same value. The dual rate tables on the other hand allow for the investment of a sinking fund at a lower rate than the discount rate. This is because the sinking fund element is actual rather than notional in some types of property transaction, requiring a low rate appropriate to risk-free gilt-edged securities. Using the YP table to find the present value of an annuity which exactly equates the present value of a series of single future sums, however, does not make use of the dual rate concept, the value of each r being identical therefore. This is known as single rate years purchase. YP may be assumed to be single rate whenever it is referred to in this book unless otherwise qualified.

As with the PV tables, separate YP tables are available which allow for *the effect of income tax*, this time on that part of the income used to provide the annual sinking fund instalment. But the student need not despair at the mention of yet another set of tables since, like the PV (tax) and the dual-rate YP (no tax allowance) tables, the YP (tax) tables are not appropriate to our present use of valuation tables, and the introduction of taxation into the calculations is in any case dealt with in later chapters.

Initial and annual costs

Returning now to the present value of annual running costs, these may be expressed as follows:

$$PV = C_a(YPF)$$

where C_a is a cost per annum and YPF is the years purchase factor. So that the PV of a project containing initial, running and periodic costs will be:

$$PV = C_0 + C_a(YPF) + \sum(PVF \times C_p)$$

it being recalled that C_0 represents initial costs (in year 0), and C_p a cost at some future period.

The following example illustrates the use of the YP table in solving a simple problem involving initial and running costs only.

EXAMPLE 2

Problem

It is proposed by the designer at cost-checking stage to substitute double for single glazing. The cost of the double glazing is estimated to be £3900, as against the £1050 shown for single glazing in the cost plan.

The heating engineer estimates however that the substitution of double glazing will reduce running costs by £250 per annum.

Calculate the ultimate saving, if any, which would be achieved over a period of 30 years life of the building if double glazing were to be selected by the designer.

The cost plan allowance for heating installation with single glazing is £10 450. If double glazing were selected, this would be reduced to £8230.

Assume a discount rate of 7 per cent, years purchase for a given period on a 7 per cent basis (single rate) being as follows:

Yrs	YPF
5	4·100
10	7·024
15	9·108
20	10·594
25	11·654
30	12·409
40	13·332
50	13·801

Solution

(*a*) *Single glazing*   £
   Initial costs:
   Glazing   1 050
   Heating   10 450

   Annual costs: £250 pa extra
   PV of £250 pa for 30 years
   = 250 × 12·409   3 102
                                                          ———————
   PV of single glazing   £14 602

(*b*) *Double glazing*
   Initial costs:
   Glazing   3 900
   Heating   8 230   12 130
                                                          ———————
   Ultimate saving with double glazing   £2 472

Discount notation

We have examined some of the algebraic formulae used in discounting, and made use of 'table-directive' formulae to direct our minds to the use of correct tables in lieu of algebraic substitution and arithmetic. As a way of indicating what we are doing when we use the tables themselves, we may use what is known as discount notation, and this may be found useful as an additional aide-memoire. The following modified version may be recommended in this connection.

Vertical lines are brackets enclosing an investment (usually designated by the letter E) with subscripts representing the year or years in which the investment takes place. Outside the brackets are placed superscripts representing year numbers and subscripts representing rates of interest. Thus an investment (cash flow) occurring in year 5 of a project and to be discounted to year 0 at the rate r would be written:

$$\left.{}^{0}_{r}\right| E_5 \left|\right.$$

the 0 and r being on the left-hand side so as to indicate the process of discounting backwards in time. The directive to compound E forwards from year 0 to year 5 at the rate r would be written:

$$E_0 \left|{}^{5}_{r}\right.$$

In this way the present value of a project can be represented as:

$$\left| E_0 \right| + {}^{0}_{r}\left| E \atop 1(1)n \right| + \sum {}^{0}_{r}\left| E_p \right|$$
$$\quad (a) \qquad\qquad (b) \qquad\qquad (c)$$

where (a) = initial costs
       (b) = annual costs
       (c) = periodic costs

The annual costs are subscripted $1(1)n$ representing their occurrence every one year from year 1 to year n, the (1) representing the interval between successive cash flows. The periodic costs (c) are shown as E_p representing an investment at a certain period of time, discounted to year 0 at the rate r and then summated with like cash flows.

This notation, like the table-directive formulae, will be found useful in expressing discounting operations in connexion with both the PV and the AE methods of analysis, and also for yield analysis operations.

Net present value

It will be apparent that when evaluating building projects which are to be let or leased out to occupiers, or disposed of by sale, there will be income to take into account as well as costs. The full implications of this will be taken into consideration in later chapters. For the time being however it should be noted that where positive cash flows occur when using the PV method of comparison, these do not invalidate the method, but are simply discounted in the usual way and given the opposite sign to the negative ones, the costs. The present value of the project then takes the form:

$$\text{NPV} = \sum_r {}^0 \left| P \right| - \sum_r {}^0 \left| N \right|$$

where P is a positive cash flow and N a negative cash flow, and NPV the *net present value*.

In general, the project with the highest NPV is the most profitable, and it is possible to rank projects in order of profitability by this means. However, the use of a *profitability index* may be desirable here. This is needed when comparing projects of differing sizes and lengths of life. The present value of a project tells us the present equivalent of its total cost, but does not of itself tell us anything about the length of time over which the costs are spread. Neither does the NPV, being a single positive or negative sum of money, tell us anything about the length of time over which the profit is made, or even how long is necessary before any profit is made at all. If the NPV is positive, a profit of some kind is made in the end; and if negative, a loss is incurred. If zero, one breaks even eventually.

By dividing the present value of the cash flows by the investment we can obtain an index number, and this profitability index will enable us to rank projects in order of their ultimate profitability in terms of income compared with expenditure. However, having roughly established a pecking-order of projects in this way (for further discussion of ranking order see Chapter 4), we may then need to inspect the cash flows and calculate their payback periods in order to compare the lengths of time before each project covers its cost and starts to make a profit; the actual degree of profitability in terms of yield percentage being determined by means of the IRR method, dealt with in Chapter 6. Meanwhile, it is not proposed to deal in any greater depth with the NPV method at this stage. The concept of net present value will arise again and will be the subject of further discussion later.

One advantage of the PV method of comparison is that it can be used to rank projects without taking income into account, which makes it especially useful for cost-in-use studies at design stage. It also has the merit of being simple in operation, and easy to interpret; and, as we shall see, it forms the basis of other methods of appraisal. These include the AE method, which also has the advantage of being a system which does not of necessity postulate any positive cash flows, with the added advantage of providing information in a way which is often more convenient and meaningful than is a lump sum present value. This is the method which will be examined in the next chapter.

Chapter 3
The annual equivalent method

When we are contemplating the purchase of a new car, we generally take into account the running costs and depreciation, as well as the initial cost of buying the car and putting it on the road. The annual costs of tax and insurance, maintenance and repairs, garaging etc, are borne in mind when deciding on a suitable model, as is the petrol consumption. We should perhaps do a PV appraisal before buying our next car, and back our hazy idea of the relative ultimate costs of the various models we have in mind by hard data! But in practice we do not usually bother to regulate our personal affairs so meticulously as this. After all, if the car proves too uneconomical we can usually get rid of it fairly quickly, having learned our lesson the hard way.

Supposing however we did require some kind of fairly accurate cost appraisal of our car project, would the PV method be suitable in fact? There would be no positive cash flows to consider (unless we were proposing to hire the car out or run a taxi service) so that unlike methods requiring an income, the PV method would certainly be a workable system for car purchase. We could simply use the formula:

$$PV = C_0 + C_a(YPF) + \Sigma(PVF \times C_p)$$

where C_0 = the purchase price

C_a = the estimated annual running costs including tax, insurance, petrol etc

C_p = the estimated periodic costs of major overhauls and repairs.

Having done our discounting, we should then have a lump sum figure for each car, representing its present value, and these we could list in ranking order, the lowest representing the ultimate best buy.

To make the figures comparable we should need to select the same 'life' for each car, but in fact some would perhaps last longer than others, being of better quality in the first place. However, we could compensate for this by selecting the shortest life and discounting the resale value of the other cars as positive cash flows, to be deducted from their present values. Notice that 'depreciation', regarded as an annual 'cost', does not figure in our calculations at all. This is because annual depreciation is not a cash flow, and only cash flows count in discounted cash flow exercises. The depreciation is purely notional until the vehicle is actually sold at a price lower than that for which it was bought (that is, its *residual* value); the concept of 'writing down' the value of the asset annually being merely a book-keeping device for keeping account of a company's probable assets—hence the term 'book value' to denote the written-down value of an asset. Thus in DCF analysis the concept of annual depreciation is only valid in the context of tax allowance (since tax is an actual cash flow) and this is dealt with in Chapter 7.

Having thus discounted the estimated residual values of the cars and adjusted each PV accordingly, we may select the car with the lowest PV knowing this to be the ultimate best buy on the evidence of the data available. But we cannot readily judge its worth against current or future expenditure, or against the alternative of, say, hiring a car instead. What we really need to know, in order to assess our financial ability to run a particular car, is not its notional comparative cost but its equivalent *annual* cost, which we can divide by twelve and compare with our net monthly income. This is more especially the case when we recall the fact that many if not most cars are nowadays bought on hire purchase or with the aid of a bank loan, so that even the initial cost (less deposit) is in fact a monthly (= annual) cost instead of a lump sum present-day cost.

This is equally the case with real property. Because the initial cost of land and building is normally mortgaged or acquired by means of loan finance, it is often more appropriate to calculate the total annual costs rather than the present-day costs, especially since the former can then be directly set against the annual rents generated, or the possible alternative of leasing instead of buying for example. This is known as the annual equivalent (AE) method of comparison.

To arrive at the annual equivalent of the initial costs of a construction project, we need to consider two kinds of cost, namely site costs and building costs.

Site costs

A freehold site is not a 'wasting asset', ie, it is not subject to wear and tear over a period of time. Quite the opposite in fact, since land values tend to rise, often very sharply, over the life of a project. This is a process of inflation however, which is considered separately, and will be dealt with later. In any case, it only affects the residual value (and consequent capital gains tax situation where applicable).

Since land is not a wasting asset (unless possessed in leasehold) the equivalent annual cost of the site is only *the annual interest* on the money borrowed to pay for it. This is because the actual loan itself is retained in the value of the site, which in theory can be sold off at any time to repay it. In practice it is more likely to be used as security for another loan to pay off the first one. Since freehold land is held in perpetuity, this process continues indefinitely. Hence the annual equivalent of the site is the annual interest on its cost, usually taken as being the discount rate in AE analysis.

It will be appreciated that whether the money is *actually* raised by loan capital or not is really irrelevant, since paying interest on a loan is equivalent to *foregoing* interest on the same amount of money paid out in cash (though the actual *rates* of interest may differ of course).

Building costs
A building is a wasting asset, being subject to wear and tear and thus having a finite life. If we borrow money to erect a building, we shall be required to pay annual interest on it, as with the site loan above. But the building is not as asset in perpetuity, like land in fee simple. So when the time comes to repay the loan, the value of the building will be insufficient to cover the cost of loan repayment (ie, redemption). To meet this state of affairs we shall need to make provision in advance, and this is traditionally achieved by setting up a sinking fund during the life of the asset which equates the original cost by the time the value of the asset depreciates to zero, that is at the end of the project life. Thus, at any time during the life of the building, its value plus the amount accumulated in the sinking fund (SF) at that time will (approximately) equate the loan; while the value of the SF at the end of the project life will be the exact amount needed to pay back the loan and thus avoid further interest charges on a vanished asset with no further income.

To ensure that the value of the SF at redemption is equal to the initial cost of the building, it will be necessary to set aside each year an amount of money which will accumulate at compound interest to just the right amount at year n, and this can be found by the following formula:

$$ASF = \frac{r}{(1 + r)^n - 1}$$

where ASF = the annual sinking fund instalment
  n = the project life
  r = the rate of interest.

In practice we again have recourse to tables, this time the annual sinking fund (ASF) table, giving us a factor which, when multiplied by the total amount to be redeemed (in this case the cost of the building), gives the appropriate annual sinking fund instalment.

Meanwhile there is still the annual interest to pay on the loan, as in the case of the site. This interest is usually denoted as i in the formula:

$$SF + i$$

which represents sinking fund instalment plus interest, ie, the annual equivalent of the cost of building.

Annual equivalent of initial costs
To summarize so far, the annual equivalent of the initial costs of a construction project may be written as follows:

$$CS(i) + CB(SF_n + i)$$

where CS = the cost of the site
  CB = the cost of building

SF$_n$ = the sinking fund instalment necessary in order to redeem the cost of building in n years

i   = the interest rate.

Or in discount notation:

$$\left| E_r \right| + \left| E_n \right|^{\dfrac{1}{r}}_{n} + \left| E_r \right|$$

(*a*)   (*b*)   (*c*)

where (*a*) shows an annual investment of interest at the rate r, representing the site cost, and (*b*) represents an investment E in the year n (loan redemption) discounted from year 1 to year n at the rate r (SF instalments), followed by (*c*) which is the annual interest on the building loan. When E is an annual investment, the interest rate replaces the year digit inside the brackets, as shown.

It might perhaps be thought at this stage that the concept of a sinking fund is very hypothetical, because in practice sinking funds are very often not set up at all. And this is especially true in building development where the life of the project is the 'investment horizon' rather than the physical life of the building, which in any case will probably command a residual value greater than the original loan due to factors such as inflation. As E. J. Broster remarks however,* the idea of a sinking fund is largely a cost accounting fiction, but it is a convenient and useful one, and is assumed by all methods of discounting, although it is more obvious in those methods which refer specifically to a sinking fund in the calculations than in those which do not.

Annual costs

These do not require converting since they are in the form of annual costs to start with. Thus the formula for initial and annual costs becomes:

$$AE = CS(i) + CB(SF_n + i) + C_a$$

where C_a represents the annual costs of the project.

The following example illustrates a calculation of the annual equivalent costs of a project involving initial and annual costs.

EXAMPLE 3

Problem

Mr Brown owns the freehold interest in a light engineering works. He has recently purchased an adjoining freehold site for £12 000 in order to extend his premises.

Appraising Capital Works, Longman, 1968.

The estimated cost of constructing the proposed brick extension is £24 000 and the annual running costs for rates, heating, lighting, insurance, etc, including an allowance for repairs, are estimated at £3500 per annum. The building has an estimated life of 50 years.

Calculate the costs in use of this extension on a 5 per cent basis making necessary use of the following table.

Yrs	SF factor
5	0·1810
10	0·0795
15	0·0463
20	0·0302
25	0·0210
30	0·0151
40	0·0083
50	0·0048
60	0·0028

Solution

$$AE = CS(i) + CB(SF_n + i) + C_a$$

Therefore:

	£	£
Cost of site:	12 000	
AE in perpetuity:		
Interest @ 5% $\times$	0·05	
	600·00	600
Cost of building:	£24 000	
AE over 50 yrs = $SF_n + i$		
SF factor for 50 yrs	0·0048	
Interest @ 5%	0·05	
24 000 $\times$	0·0548 $=$	£1 315
Annual costs:		
Running costs £3 500 pa		3 500
Annual equivalent costs-in-use		£5 415

Note 1. For the purpose of this exercise the estimated cost of £24 000 for constructing this factory extension is assumed to include all professional fees and charges—likewise the £12 000 for land acquisition costs.

Note 2. The cost of building is assumed to be a lump sum of £24 000 expended in year 0, and redeemed by sinking fund in year 50. In practice however this initial cost is spread over a period of time by means of stage payments, which do not start until the design period is over. Thus on a major project some years may elapse between land acquisition and settlement of the final account, requiring adjustment to the appraisal as discussed later.

Periodic costs

Certain maintenance costs etc, will occur periodically rather than annually, as we have already noted in the case of the PV method of comparison. These may be costs occurring at regular intervals (eg, decorations every five years) or single sums of money for such things as alterations, or renewal of part of the fabric or services. In the case of the PV method these sums are discounted individually to year 0 and aggregated with the initial costs, recurring sums allowing of PV factor summation as a short-cut device, as we have seen. To find the annual equivalent of these periodic (that is, non-annual) costs we can also make use of short-cut devices, and it will be convenient to divide periodic costs into four categories for this purpose, namely:

(1) differing magnitudes (or a single sum)
(2) uniform sums
(3) uniform sums and periods with no final payment
(4) ditto but with final uniform payment.

Each of these will now be dealt with in turn.

Periodic costs comprising individual sums

The term 'periodic costs' is used to mean any cost (other than initial costs) which is not a recurring annual cost. Such periodic costs may be in the form of one single sum occurring at a point along the time-scale of the project, or a number of such sums. Taking the case of a single sum (eg, for renewing the roof coverings after twenty-five years), the problem is to find its annual equivalent cost.

Now we have seen that the annual equivalent of a single sum occurring in year 0 (eg, the initial cost of building) is found by the formula:

$$CB(SF_n + i)$$

where CB, the cost of building, represents a wasting asset. Periodic costs will also be wasting assets, so these must be similarly treated, after first being moved back down the time-scale to year 0 by means of discounting. Thus we first find the PV of the period cost and then spread it forwards over the life of the project in the form of annual payments. If there is more than one such periodic cost we can add their present values together and convert the total amount in one operation. Hence if C_p represents any periodic cost, we may write:

$$AE = \Sigma(PVF \times C_p)(SF_n + i)$$

as the formula for finding the annual equivalent of all periodic costs. In discount notation this would be represented as: s

$$1 \left| \sum_{r}^{0} \left| E_p \right| \right|_{r}^{n} + \left| E_r \right|$$

$$(a) \qquad\qquad (b)$$

where (a) is the sum of the periodic costs E_p discounted to year 0 at the rate r and then accumulated forwards from year 1 to year n by means of a sinking fund at the rate r, and (b) is the annual interest on the loan.

Periodic uniform sums
Periodic costs are often in the form of recurring identical sums, and in such cases we may summate the PV factors instead of discounting each sum separately, as when using the PV method of comparison. The formula then becomes:

$$AE = C_p(\Sigma PVF)(SF_n + i)$$

which will result in a saving in arithmetic.

Uniform sums and periods
If both the sums and also the periods are uniform (eg, redecorating every five years at a cost of £2000) then an additional simplification may be made, resulting in what can prove to be a considerable further saving in arithmetic in certain cases. The formula is as follows:

$$AE = C_p(SF_p - SF_n)$$

where SF_p is the sinking fund factor over the uniform period, and SF_n the sinking fund factor over the life of the project. This will be made clear by an example, but meanwhile this formula can be justified as follows.

If a recurring cost is discounted over the interval of time back to its previous occurrence, the resultant annual equivalent over the interval will apply to all of the other identical intervals. But since there is no expenditure occurring at the beginning of the first interval (if there was, it would be an initial cost and not a periodic cost) the annual equivalent in respect of the first interval (that is, period) must be deducted from the result. In order to achieve this, the AE of the first period must be computed over the entire life of the project before it can be deducted from the AE over the interval, since this is also represented as occurring annually over the entire project life. Hence:

$$AE = C_p(SF_p + i) - C_p(SF_n + i)$$
$$= C_p(SF_p) - C_p(SF_n)$$
$$= C_p(SF_p - SF_n)$$

It should be especially noted that this formula will only apply provided the following two conditions are present:

(1) *End period uniform.* The end (final) period must be uniform. That is to say, the time interval between the last payment and year n must be the same as that between any two successive payments. Thus painting (say) every 5 years during a 30-year life would come within the conditions. Painting every 7 years during the same life would not however, because this would leave an interval of 2 years instead of 7 between the last payment and year n.

(2) *No final payment.* There must be no final payment due in year n. The formula presumes the last maintenance charge to occur one period prior to the end of the project life, thus making it suitable, for example, for freehold properties presumed demolished in year n.

Full repairing leases
In cases where a final uniform payment needs to be made in year n, at the end of the project life, yet a further simplification can take place, because each uniform period now ends with a payment, including the last period. Thus the annual equivalent for the entire project life becomes the same as the annual equivalent of one payment over one period; the periods then being placed end-to-end evenly over the project life, so to speak. Thus the equation for the AE of the periodic costs over the project life now reduces to:

$$AE = C_p(SF_p)$$

Annuity tables
When calculating the annual equivalent of a wasting asset by use of the formula SF + i, it is customary to look up the annual sinking fund factor and then add interest, as we have seen. Where the interest rate is the same as the sinking fund rate however, reference may be made instead to the tables of *annuity one pound will purchase* (*single rate*). This is in effect an annual equivalent table, being a combination of sinking fund and interest. Dual rate annuity tables are also available, *Parry's* giving a flat $2\frac{1}{2}$ per cent sinking fund rate with interest rates from 3 to 16 per cent.

The *mortgage instalment table* also gives SF + i, but in the form of monthly instead of annual equivalents, and the factors represent one hundred pounds instead of one pound.

Summary of AE formulae
Before giving a worked example involving periodic costs, it might perhaps be desirable to summarize briefly the table-directive formulae discussed in this chapter in connection with the AE method.

AE FORMULAE SUMMARY

(A) Initial and annual costs:

$$AE = CS(i) + CB(SF_n + i) + C_a$$

(B) Periodic costs:
  (1) differing magnitudes (or single sum)

$$AE = \sum(PVF \times C_p)(SF_n + i)$$

  (2) uniform sums

$$AE = C_p(\sum PVF)(SF_n + i)$$

  (3) uniform sums and periods
    (*a*) no final payment:

$$AE = C_p(SF_p - SF_n)$$

  (*b*) final uniform payment:

$$AE = C_p(SF_p)$$

The following example illustrates the calculation of the annual equivalent of a project involving periodic as well as annual and initial costs.

_____

EXAMPLE 4

Problem

A new office block is to be erected by a developer who already owns the site. Calculate its annual equivalent cost, using the following data.

Construction costs	= £200 000
Running costs	= £10 000 per annum
Redecoration costs	= £15 000 every 5 years
Renewal of roof coverings	= £50 000 after 30 years
Life of the project	= 50 years
Interest rate	= 7 per cent

Present value factors of £1 and sinking fund factors for the redemption of £1 capital invested at 7 per cent interest are as follows:

Yrs	SF factor	PV factor
5	0·1739	0·7130
10	0·0724	0·5083
20	0·0244	0·2584
30	0·0106	0·1314
40	0·0050	0·0668
50	0·0025	0·0340

Solution

		£		
Cost of building:		200 000		
$AE = CB(SF_n + i)$				
SF over 50 years		0·0025		
Interest @ 7%		0·07		
		——		
200 000	×	0·0725	=	£14 500
Annual costs:				
Running costs £10 000 pa				£10 000
Periodic costs:				
Redecorations every 5 yrs		15 000		
$AE = C_p(SF_p - SF_n)$				
SF over 5 yrs		0·1739		
SF over 50 yrs		0·0025		
		——		
15 000	×	0·1714	=	2 571
Renewals after 30 yrs		50 000		
$AE = (PVF \times C_p)(SF_n + i)$				
$= (0·1314 \times 50\,000)(0·0725)$			=	476
				——
Annual equivalent cost				£27 547

Chapter 4
Feasibility Studies

We have examined the PV and the AE methods of appraisal and seen how these can be used to reduce the initial, annual, and periodic costs of a construction project to a common denominator for the purpose of comparison. We may wish to compare the resultant present value with the PV of an alternative project; to compare the annual equivalent of building a factory with the annual rent payable if we lease one instead; with the income if we ourselves let it to others; or the price if we sell it. Or we may wish to establish the ranking-order of a number of possible projects. But before carrying out any such feasibility study with the aid of discounted cash flow systems it will be necessary to estimate cash flows as accurately as possible.

The fixing of positive cash flows such as estimated income from renting or selling is properly the province of the professional valuer, who should be consulted whenever necessary. The prediction of the negative cash flows is the function of the building economist who, as a qualified quantity surveyor and cost planner, will be an expert in the field of preliminary estimate preparation. Such preliminary estimates are normally thought of as being estimates of the contract price of the building with the addition of quantity surveyor's and design fees. But the initial capital cost of a project to a developer will need to include far more than this, because there are land acquisition costs to consider, as well as other possible outgoings in connection with the project. Then again there is the question of the annual and periodic costs to take into account, and before the cash flows for these can be fixed it will be necessary to review the proposed project to establish the various cost categories likely to arise, so that their amounts and position on the time-scale can be estimated.

From the point of view of discounting operations we have divided costs into initial, annual and periodic. But when analysing a project for the purpose of establishing its cash flow 'profile' at feasibility stage, it will be convenient to establish cost categories appropriate to their detailed function; in other words to find out what has got to be paid for at each stage of the project. Ideally we need a checklist of cost categories which go to make up the cash flow profiles of development projects, to help ensure that possible cash flows are not overlooked in practice, or necessary ones omitted by students in examinations. Meanwhile the following notes give an indication of cost categories which need to be considered when making up the negative cash flows for a building project appraisal.

CAPITAL COSTS

Land acquisition

In addition to the purchase price of the land, the following outgoings also need to be considered:

(*a*) solicitors' fees
(*b*) Land Registry fees
(*c*) stamp duty
(*d*) valuers' fees
(*e*) consultancy fees

Solicitors' fees for conveyancing may be based on a sliding scale which is in existence at the time of writing, but in future may be based on the amount of work involved rather than on the value of the land. The scale fees are higher for dealing with unregistered land than for registered land. Owing to the fact that fees may be charged on an *ad hoc* basis it is advisable to consult a solicitor regarding legal fees in any individual case before deciding on the cash flow allowance. But as a very rough indication indeed, the current scale fees in respect of unregistered land amount to approximately one per cent on a £10 000 estate, falling to about half per cent on £100 000 and over. In the case of registered land these fees would be reduced by almost half.

Land Registry fees are in addition to conveyancing fees, and again depend upon the circumstances of the case. At time of writing the registry of land has been temporarily suspended in some areas of the country, no fees being payable. Where fees are compulsory however, the purchaser of any unregistered land becomes liable for Land Registry fees currently amounting to £14 on a £10 000 estate. If the land is already registered before purchase, the fees are higher, but still only amount to £25 on £10 000, which for the purpose of cash flow analysis may at present be considered fairly negligible.

Stamp duty is payable in addition on transfer of landed property, but only on estates exceeding a minimum value (£10 000 at time of writing). Above that figure, stamp duty is currently charged at one per cent.

Here it must be further stressed that the figures mentioned in the above section are subject to alteration and should not be used without prior consultation with a legal advisor. They are given here only as a rough indication of their relative importance in relation to cost appraisal work.

In certain circumstances the services of a valuer might be retained to value the site before acquisition, in which case a valuation fee may have to be allowed for. It is also possible that advice may be sought from an architect, engineer or surveyor as to the suitability of the proposed site for the type of development envisaged prior to purchase, and any professional fees incurred in this respect should not be overlooked.

Site preparation

Having acquired the land, additional expenditure by way of site preparation may be necessary before the main contractor can start work. Site preparation is divided into two main categories by N. Lichfield,* namely legal and physical, and the following checklist may be helpful in setting the cash flows.

(1) Legal preparation of site:
   (*a*) closing rights of way
   (*b*) discharging restrictive covenants
   (*c*) buying out easements, or acquiring them over other land
   (*d*) redeeming tithe redemption annuities or land tax
   (*e*) adjusting boundaries with adjoining owners.

(2) Physical preparation of site:
   (*a*) demolition and site clearance
   (*b*) landscape architect's (or engineer's) fees
   (*c*) approach roads, main sewers, water, gas and electricity service mains.

Initial cost of building

When allowing for the initial capital cost of erecting the building, the following three main cost categories call for consideration:

(1) the contract sum
(2) quantity surveyor's and design fees
(3) developer's profit.

To the estimated contract price will need to be added an allowance for quantity surveyor's and design fees, which will normally be based on the official scale of fees obtainable from the RICS and RIBA. The possibility of consulting engineer's fees should not be overlooked, and these should be added to the architect's fees if they are likely to be incurred. The Association of Consulting Engineers Conditions of Engagement and Scales of Fees will probably be relevant in this connexion.

When considering the contract price and professional fees, the interest on capital used during the construction period is sometimes thought of as part of the initial cost of building. Interest on capital used at site acquisition and preparation stages falls into the same category of expenditure however, and in any case this outgoing may be a notional 'opportunity' cost rather than an actual cash flow. It is best thought of as an ancillary discounting procedure rather than an initial cost in its own right, and is therefore dealt with later in this chapter under the separate heading of 'pre-project finance'.

Economics of Planned Development, Estates Gazette, 1956.

Developer's profit on the other hand is probably best treated as a negative cash flow, passing out from the project and into the pocket of the developer. It is usually thought of as applying to private enterprise development only; but it should not be forgotten that in certain circumstances financial profitability may be justifiably considered as at least one of the criteria to be employed when appraising public development also. However that may be, profit (in private enterprise) is traditionally defined as 'the reward for taking risk', and the outlay incurred by a private developer may be a very heavy one. The degree of entrepreneurial risk involved in laying out large capital sums will of course vary with the circumstances, and will be carefully assessed by the developer himself and his financial backers. Quite apart from the ultimate profitability of the project, the developer may well require an initial return, to cover his entrepeneurial risk, in the form of a difference between the initial cost of the project and its market value before it starts to earn an income from, say, rents. This entrepreneurial profit for initial risk is in addition to the profit obtained from investment in the project as a going concern, and is best thought of as part of the initial cost of development, ie, as a negative cash flow occurring in year 0.

According to Lichfield, a common allowance for developers profit is between 5 per cent and 20 per cent of the total initial cost, excluding land, or of the values to be created.

Disposal expenses

If the development is to be let or sold on completion a negative cash flow allowance should be made in respect of *agent's commission*, which includes advertising expenses. The current RICS fees for sale of freehold property are on a sliding scale, a rough indication of which is: just over two per cent on £10 000, falling to slightly over one-and-a-half per cent on £100 000.

The normal fee for letting of unfurnished premises is ten per cent of one year's rent, but as with the fee for selling, circumstances alter cases and these figures are intended as a very rough guide only, especially since the fees in any specific instance are now subject to negotiation.

Disposal expenses may be incurred at the commencement of a project (speculative development) as part of the capital costs, or in connection with the disposal of the asset at the end of the project life, or both. In addition to the agent's commission, they will also incur a certain amount of legal fees and stamp duties on contracts or leases.

RUNNING COSTS

In April 1971 the Building Maintenance Cost Information Service (BMCIS) was established, following a pilot study carried out by the University of Bath. At the invitation of the Department of the Environment (formerly the MPBW) which financed the pilot study, the control of the BMCIS was taken over by the RICS, which published an introductory article* on its scope in 1972. This gave an interesting classification of the 'scope of property administration' as follows.

PROPERTY OCCUPANCY COSTS

(A) Personal services:
    (1) estate management
    (2) porterage

(B) Running costs:
    (1) maintenance costs:
        (*a*) fabric maintenance
        (*b*) mechanical and engineering maintenance
        (*c*) cleaning
    (2) operating costs:
        (*a*) servicing
        (*b*) fuel and power.

B. E. Drake† however uses a classification which groups costs other than capital costs into:
    (1) maintenance of facilities, including restoration
    (2) operating costs, including fuel, lighting, cleaning, porterage etc
    (3) alterations, including improvements and adaptations.

On the other hand, Lichfield divides annual costs into (*a*) occupation expenses and (*b*) ownership expenses; and it is suggested that for the purpose of DCF analysis this may be a useful concept. If we think of maintenance costs as being outgoings in respect of redecorations, repairs, renewals and alterations ('maintaining' the usage), and of cleaning as an operating cost like servicing and porterage, then our grouping can be adjusted to fit the annual/periodic discounting classification. It will then be appropriate to refer to *annual running costs*, as opposed to *periodic maintenance costs*, giving us a grouping as follows:

    (1) Annual running costs:
        (*a*) occupation costs
        (*b*) ownership costs

    (2) Periodic maintenance costs

It will be appreciated that this grouping, while useful in the present con-

---

*D. Robertson, 'The Building Maintenance Cost Information Service', *The Chartered Surveyor*, February, 1972.
†'The Economics of Maintenance', *The Quantity Surveyor*, July, 1969.

text, may not be strictly valid for all building types or necessarily convenient for all purposes. For example, in the case of public buildings such as schools, the separation of ownership and occupation costs may not be meaningful, and maintenance costs may be partly annual and partly periodic. Again, for the purpose of cost accounting a sub-division into BMCIS elements is preferable, and a list of these is given later in this chapter. Maintenance costs may be either occupation or ownership costs, or split between the two, as when external painting is the owner's and internal painting the tenant's responsibility.

Occupation costs
These fall upon the owner-occupier, lessee or tenant and may comprise any or all of the following:

(1)   rates (including water rates)
(2)   insurance
(3)   cleaning
(4)   servicing of mechanical and engineering equipment
(5)   fuel and power
(6)   gardening and porterage etc.

Porterage etc may include the cost of caretakers, boilermen, odd-job men, security services, laundry services (eg, the provision of toilet towels) and rubbish disposal expenses, as well as the cost of porters.

These costs are occupation costs in the sense that they might not arise if the building is not occupied, or may only arise in part if the building is part-occupied. Although these outgoings fall upon the occupier, any or all of them may, by agreement, be included in the rent of course; and in some instances, as in the case of rates on domestic property on tenancy agreements, this is a commonplace arrangement.

Insurance of the fabric, as opposed to the contents, is probably best regarded as an ownership expense, though this again might be included in the terms of the lease.

Telephone rental charges are another item payable by the occupier; but although these are increasing they are usually regarded as negligible for cash flow purposes, or alternatively, (like the call charges themselves) as not chargeable to the running costs of the building.

Ownership costs
Rates may now be levied on vacant property in certain instances and are therefore included as both an occupation and an ownership cost. Insurance comes into this category also, since insurance of the fabric will be required regardless of whether all or part of the building is occupied. Fire insurance must cover the cost of rebuilding, not the historic cost of the premises. It is usual for an estimate of cost for fire insurance purposes to exclude the cost of substructure and drainage.

Ownership costs may include the following:
(1) rates
(2) insurance
(3) estate management
(4) land tax
(5) tithe redemption annuity
(6) voids.

Estate management costs include rent collection, tenancy renewal, and repair and maintenance management. The fees for estate management vary according to the type of property and the amount of work involved from anything between about 2 and 10 per cent of the income generated by the property.

The allowance for *voids* is sometimes made in the case of rented flats, shops, etc. This is equivalent to making a deduction from the total rents received on account of vacancies due to changes of tenancy or other unforeseen circumstances. It is often convenient to regard it as an ownership cost: one which is, incidentally, tax-free in the sense of foregoing a taxable revenue.

MAINTENANCE COSTS

Total expenditure in the United Kingdom on the maintenance and repair of buildings is currently in the region of £2000 million per annum and, according to C. D. Browning,* more than one third of building labour throughout the country is permanently employed on maintenance and repair work. These figures give an indication of the importance of maintenance costs in the national economy. But from the point of view of the building economist engaged in the cost appraisal of individual projects, or design solutions of cost-planning elements, the setting of cash flows will depend on estimation of the lives and renewal costs of the various materials and components which go to make up the building.

Cost research is not a field with which this present book is directly concerned, and the work of forecasting the timing and magnitude of cash flows in respect of either capital or maintenance costs is a matter for the trained cost consultant, making use of his own cost library, supplemented as necessary by the Building Cost Information and the Building Maintenance Cost Information Services. The following brief notes will therefore be confined to definitions and classification of maintenance costs, and their relationship with capital costs.

Maintenance cost categories
If we think of maintenance as 'maintaining the usage of', we can use the term to include redecorations, repairs, renewals and alterations.

Building Economics and Cost Planning, Batsford, 1961.

Redecorations, repairs and renewals are due to wear and tear on the fabric and services, maintenance being therefore a process of 'constantly repairing the ravages of time', to borrow a phrase from Southwell,* who points out that true reparative maintenance would depend upon the building being constructed of replaceable units, eg, roof tiles, which could be replaced indefinitely, the building ultimately becoming like a knife which has had several new handles and one or two new blades! Because this is not in fact the case however, the ravages of time are not in fact fully repaired, and thus a building has a finite life. But as Southwell goes on to suggest, the life of a building is governed by economic trends which override its ability to withstand wear and tear. One such factor would be obsolescence due to social and economic change—as when the value of the site becomes greater than that of the building on it. This is typified by the case of detached houses on urban sites which are demolished to make way for high-rise flats or office blocks. Therefore we are only actually concerned with the maintenance occurring within the *planned functional life* of the building, from inception to the *investment horizon* of the project.

In addition to redecorations, repairs and renewals, there might be a change of function envisaged before the investment horizon is reached, in which case alterations to change the use of the building (or to improve its present use) will enable its life to be preserved, in the sense of escaping demolition due to obsolescence. Thus we could classify maintenance cost categories as follows:

(1) Preservation:
    (*a*) redecorations
    (*b*) repairs
    (*c*) renewals

(2) Adaptation:
    (*a*) improvements
    (*b*) alterations.

Maintenance and capital costs

The timing and magnitude of cash flows for maintenance work will depend mainly on the materials and components involved in the design-solution of each element. It will be found that there is often an inverse relationship between the initial cost and the subsequent maintenance cost of a particular item: the higher the first cost, the lower the subsequent maintenance charges, and vice versa. This is to be expected, since a better quality product is likely to cost more than a poor quality one (by and large you get what you pay for, as the saying goes); and it is likely to last longer. (It does not follow from this that future running costs can always be reduced by spending more money initially. The reader will appreciate that the cause of building failures and the incidence of occupancy costs is much more complex than this.) In other cases

*J. Southwell, *Total Building Cost Appraisal*, RICS, 1967.

annual running costs might be altered by a change of design which will also alter the initial costs, as in the case of a change from single to double glazing which makes a saving in the running costs of heating.

Now we have seen that it is the purpose of the PV and the AE methods to evaluate such alternatives by reducing them to a common denominator. When comparing results however, there may be factors affecting the balance between maintenance costs (and for that matter, running costs) and capital costs which will modify or invalidate a simple PV or AE ranking. Some of these factors will tend to favour a relatively low initial cost and some relatively low maintenance costs, as follows.

(1) *Low maintenance costs.* Maintenance costs cannot normally be paid for out of mortgage, and where ample initial funds are available a low-maintenance design may be desirable at the expense of higher initial costs, especially since future maintenance expenses will be subject to inflation, unlike mortgage repayments. Similarly, in the case of public works, maintenance costs might not be subject to the same exchequer grants available to capital costs.

Relatively expensive (and consequently maintenance-free) materials may be dictated by their prestige value or architectural merit (cheap materials tend to look cheap); or may be used in positions where repair is thought to be unduly expensive or inconvenient; or for civic or other buildings erected for posterity.

(2) *High maintenance costs.* Relatively high maintenance costs may be tolerated where initial costs need to be kept to a minimum, for example because of limited mortgage facilities. Then again, in some instances (eg, speculative development) the maintenance costs will not be borne by the developer at all. In other types of development, where early obsolescence is envisaged, the consequently short project life may render maintenance costs negligible even with the cheapest of materials. Finally, tax relief on maintenance charges where none exists on capital outlay will favour low first-cost design solutions. However, a higher rate of value added tax on repair work than on new construction would tend to have the reverse effect.

BMCIS elements

A useful comprehensive checklist of possible running and maintenance costs is given in Section D of the Building Maintenance Cost Information Service, dealing with Occupancy Cost Analyses. Here a standard list of elements is given, into which an annual financial statement of occupancy costs is to be divided for the purpose of recording actual maintenance and running costs of various types of buildings. There are nine elements, sub-divided into thirty-three sub-elements as follows:

4

0. *Improvements and Adaptations.*

1. *Decoration*
1.1 External decoration
1.2 Internal decoration

2. *Fabric*
2.1 External walls
2.2 Roofs
2.3 Other structural items
2.4 Fittings and fixtures
2.5 Internal finishes

3. *Services*
3.1 Plumbing and internal drainage
3.2 Heating and ventilating
3.3 Lifts and escalators
3.4 Electric power and lighting
3.5 Other mechanical and electrical services

4. *Cleaning*
4.1 Windows
4.2 External surfaces
4.3 Internal

5. *Utilities*
5.1 Gas
5.2 Electricity
5.3 Fuel oil
5.4 Solid fuel
5.5 Water rates
5.6 Effluents and drainage charges

6. *Administrative costs*
6.1 Services attendants
6.2 Laundry
6.3 Porterage
6.4 Security
6.5 Rubbish disposal
6.6 Property management

7. *Overheads*
7.1 Property insurance
7.2 Rates

8. *External works*
8.1 Repairs and decoration
8.2 External services
8.3 Cleaning
8.4 Gardening

This list of elements separates repair work under the three main headings of Fabric, Services and External works, and the decoration of any external areas is also separated out under External works. The cost of fuel and power is grouped together under Utilities, which also includes water rates, it will be noted, as well as possible charges for removal of effluents or drainage wastes, though the cost of drainage *repairs* would be listed under External services. The costs relating to boilermen, caretakers, etc, are dealt with under sub-element 6.1, Services attendants.

For further details regarding element definitions and principles of analysis the reader is referred to Section D of the Building Maintenance Cost Information Service, published by the RICS.

PRE-PROJECT FINANCE

We now turn to another aspect of the cash flow profile of a typical proposed project undergoing a feasibility study, namely the timing and manipulation of cash flows occurring prior to year 0.

In the examples already given, it has been assumed for the sake of simplicity that the cost of building is a lump sum expended in year 0; but as indicated in a previous chapter, the initial cost of building is in practice spread over a period of time by means of stage payments. Also, a time period will elapse between site acquisition and commencement of the contract period. Since the cash flows involved in these capital costs are relatively large, it will usually be desirable to make allowance in the discounting for these factors by placing land acquisition at the beginning of the time-scale and spreading the cost of building over the contract period.

This could be done by making year 0 the year of the first cash flow (eg, land acquisition) and arranging the rest of the time-scale accordingly, onwards to year n at the end of the investment horizon. However it is generally more convenient to regard year 0 as the year in which the project *starts earning an income*, ie, at contract completion date. This convention has the advantage (*a*) that the time-scale does not have to be shifted to deal with the problem and (*b*) that year 0 can then remain the conventional base-date for the purposes of corporation tax and investment incentives etc, explained in a later chapter.

Compounding to year nought
If year 0 is deemed to represent contract completion date, then the term 'present value' means the value at that particular point in time. Any point in time could be selected as the 'present' in a project as far as discounting is concerned, provided a similar point is chosen for all projects being compared; and there is no intrinsic virtue in the date of land acquisition as a candidate for the ever-present 'now'. However, if we select year 0 as being other than the time of the first cash flow, we shall obviously need to

translate the cash flows prior to year 0 forwards instead of backwards in order to find their 'present' values. Cash flows occurring before year 0 will thus need to be 'compounded' forwards to find their terminal value at year 0, which will then become their present value. It will be recalled that the formula for finding the terminal value of one pound after n years is:

$$TV = (1 + r)^n$$

which, as we have seen, is the reciprocal of the formula for finding the present value. The compound interest table giving us the factor with which to multiply the principal to obtain the TV is called the *amount of pound* table in *Parry's*. Therefore the appropriate table-directive formula for compounding forwards is:

$$TV = S(APF)$$

where S is a sum representing the cash flow, and APF the amount of pound factor (so called because it gives the amount to which a pound will accumulate at compound interest).

The appropriate rate of interest for use when compounding forwards to year 0 in this way will depend upon the circumstances. If one thinks in terms of having to borrow the money earlier than one otherwise would because it is required earlier than year 0, then the borrowing rate would be appropriate. This represents the 'cost of financing' the project before any return is obtained on the capital outlay, the interest on finance prior to year 0. Hence the term *pre-project finance* used to describe this operation.

Nevertheless, when compounding is being used merely as a mathematical device to avoid time-scale shift, then the logical rate of interest in the case of PV and AE analysis is the *discount rate*. This will be the opportunity rate rather than the borrowing rate, ie, the cut-off rate below which the opportunity to invest money (not to borrow it) exists. However, pre-project finance is a useful term to employ in this connection, and may be divided for the purpose of DCF techniques into (*a*) land acquisition finance and (*b*) building finance.

Land acquisition finance

The purchase of the site is usually regarded as a single negative cash flow prior to year 0, though this may be split into two parts if it is thought worthwhile to separate an initial deposit to secure an option from the payment of the balance, on or before actual possession is obtained. Whether the deposit is treated as a separate cash flow will depend on the magnitude of the deposit and the length of the intervening period, but if it is so treated, each cash flow is separately compounded to year 0 and added to the present value.

Professional fees and charges in connection with site acquisition may be paid on completion of the purchase, when payment for the site is made, and if so, can be added to the cost of the land, although valuation or other consultancy fees may be paid prior to purchase completion date in some circumstances, and should then be separately compounded if substantial. Site *preparation* costs (where these do not form part of the general building contract) will be dealt with in the same manner as land acquisition or building costs.

Turning now to the mechanics of compounding a single cash flow to find its present value at year 0: there is no particular reason why the intervening period between the cash flow and year 0 should be a multiple of a twelve-month period. This brings us to the question of why *any* cash flow should be considered as occurring at the end of a twelve-month period. After all, rents are in fact paid weekly or monthly as a rule, fuel and power quarterly etc. The actual cash flows themselves, with which we are exclusively concerned, almost never occur annually in practice.

The fiction of end-year discounting is one which may be considered as acceptable for long-term capital projects such as building schemes and, according to Merrett and Sykes,* is sufficiently accurate for the appraisal of virtually all types of capital project subject to risk, if used sensibly. Monthly discounting tables are available, and monthly discounting may be more suitable for short-term projects such as dealing with a building contractor's cash flow over the construction and maintenance periods only of a contract. But feasibility studies of the project from the developer's viewpoint, with which this book is mainly concerned, are normally carried out by yearly discounting, which is considered sufficiently accurate for the purpose. One has to bear in mind, when considering the finer points of mathematical accuracy, that at feasibility stage all of the cash flows (with the possible exception of land purchase) are, after all, merely preliminary estimates.

But having said this, one must also remember that the *early* cash flows have a greater effect on the present value than do the *later* ones, owing to the very nature of discounting itself. This is just as well since the further ahead in time a cash flow occurs, the more difficult it becomes to predict its probable magnitude. But it does mean that the appraisal will benefit from a fair amount of accuracy in the setting of the initial cash flows, especially since they are relatively heavy ones. So it will pay to modify the fiction of end-year discounting in the case of the capital costs to the extent of allowing for fractional years when compounding to year 0.

For the project periods and interest rates with which we are here concerned, it will be found that the compound interest formula gives a reasonably straight-line relationship between amount of pound factors, and it is therefore common practice to use linear interpolation when calculating fractional years for pre-project finance.† This may be done by simple sub-division between two successive table factors, and if we modify the table-directive formula TV = S(APF) to read:

$$TV = S(APF_{-n})$$

The Finance and Analysis of Capital Projects, Longman, 1963.
†For a detailed discussion of the accuracy of interpolation in this context, see Merrett & Sykes, *ibid*, pp 29–32.

we can make $-n$ equal any negative year number (not necessarily an integer) and interpolate if necessary. A simple example will make this clear.

EXAMPLE 5

Problem

A building site costing £30 000 has just been acquired, and it is estimated that the date for completion of the building contract is $2\frac{1}{2}$ years hence. Calculate what the present value of the site will be at that date.

Assume the cost of the site is inclusive of all fees and charges, and that the interest rate is 8 per cent. Amount of pound factors giving compound interest rates at 8 per cent are as follows:

Yr	APF
1	1·0800
2	1·1664
3	1·2597
4	1·3605
5	1·4693

Solution

In this case we have a cash flow occurring in year minus $2\frac{1}{2}$, as shown in Figure 1.

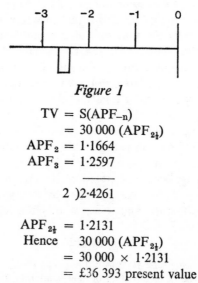

Figure 1

$$TV = S(APF_{-n})$$
$$= 30\,000\,(APF_{2\frac{1}{2}})$$
$$APF_2 = 1·1664$$
$$APF_3 = 1·2597$$

2)2·4261

$$APF_{2\frac{1}{2}} = 1·2131$$
Hence $30\,000\,(APF_{2\frac{1}{2}})$
$$= 30\,000 \times 1·2131$$
$$= £36\,393 \text{ present value}$$

Building finance

As previously indicated, the cost of building will not in fact be a single cash flow, but will be spread over a period of time. This period will extend from first stage payment (certificate number one) to settlement of the final account. Theoretically the final account should be settled by the end of the contract maintenance period, but outstanding claims or multiple variations may tend to delay the final certificate. This period of delay can hardly be foreseen at feasibility stage, however, and in any case the amount outstanding (if any) after final release of retention will represent only a very small proportion of the contract sum. This possible delay period can therefore be ignored in the feasibility study, especially since the effect of such delay will be to *increase* the NPV of the project, rather than the other way round.

The same arguments apply basically to retention held during the contract maintenance period. This will normally amount to only 5 per cent, held for six months only, and it is reasonable therefore to ignore retention money in the case of early feasibility studies of the kind under discussion. Again, one must bear in mind that at this stage the contract sum is itself in the form of a preliminary estimate.

We are left with the concept of the estimated contract sum spread over a period from first certificate to contract completion date. The cash flows will normally be monthly (under the standard form of contract) but will vary in magnitude in a fairly unpredictable way, depending on the value of work executed to date. It seems a reasonable simplification on balance of probabilities to assume the contract sum to be evenly spread. Also, a further minor concession to simplicity is often made by ignoring the interval between starting date and the first interim payment. This leaves the estimated contract sum now represented as a series of equal monthly cash flows extending from contractor's possession of the site (contract starting date) until contract completion date at year 0. Let us consider how such a series of payments may best be compounded to a terminal value.

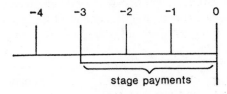

Figure 2

Compounding (or discounting) may be (*a*) end-year, (*b*) mid-year, (*c*) monthly, (*d*) continuous, (*e*) mid-point or (*f*) at any other intervals appropriate to a particular case. When considering a continuous stream of monthly payments it would seem at first glance that monthly compounding would be the obvious choice. It does not follow however that because payments are made monthly, the interest on the sums involved is necessarily calculated monthly, and a case for end-year discounting might even be made in respect of such payments. On the other hand, where cash flows arise regularly over a year, Merrett and Sykes recommend assuming that they arise mid-year, which they affirm will be found quite accurate enough for all practical purposes. This is safer than end-year compounding in the sense that the terminal value will be greater and the NPV consequently less optimistic.

Take the case of a three year contract with an estimated tender figure of £600 000, as represented in Figure 2.

With end-year discounting, assuming interest at 8 per cent, the terminal value at year 0 would be as follows:

Yr	APF		£
−2	200 000 × 1·1664	=	233 280
−1	200 000 × 1·0800	=	216 000
0	200 000 × 1·0000	=	200 000
Value at year 0		=	£649 280

With mid-year discounting on the other hand, the cash flows are presumed to occur as shown by arrows (a), (b), (c), in Figure 3.

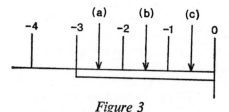

Figure 3

The terminal value is found by compounding (a) for two years, (b) for one year, and the sum of these plus (c) for the remaining half year. Now the formula for finding the equivalent half-yearly rate of interest is $\sqrt{(1 + r)} - 1$, so that the discount rate for six months equivalent to an annual rate of 8 per cent is $\sqrt{(1·108)} - 1 = 3·923$ per cent. Hence the value at year 0 by mid-year compounding would be:

	APF		£
(a)	200 000 × 1·1664	=	233 280
(b)	200 000 × 1·0800	=	216 000
			449 280
(c)	added		200 000
			649 280
		×	1·0392
Value at year 0		=	£674 732

This shows a difference of some 4 per cent increase over the end-year method.

The *mid-point* method is a simplification of the mid-year system, and has the advantage of simplicity where fractional years require to be dealt with. It assumes that a single cash flow only occurs at a point midway along the entire series of payments, as shown by the arrow in Figure 4.

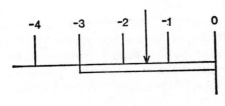

Figure 4

We revert to the method of compounding a single cash flow, as for land acquisition, thus:

$$TV = S(APF_{-n})$$
$$= 600\,000\,(APF_{1\frac{1}{2}})$$
$$APF_1 = 1 \cdot 0800$$
$$APF_2 = 1 \cdot 1664$$

$$2\,)\overline{2 \cdot 2464}$$

$$APF_{1\frac{1}{2}} = 1 \cdot 1232$$
$$\text{Hence}\quad 600\,000\,(APF_{1\frac{1}{2}})$$
$$= 600\,000 \times 1 \cdot 1232$$
$$= £673\,920$$

It can be seen that this is within a fraction of one per cent of the result achieved by the mid-year system.

When the mid-point method is adopted for pre-project building finance the formula $TV = S(APF_{-n})$ takes the form:

$$TV = S(APF_{-\frac{1}{2}n})$$

where n equals the contract period.

The following example further illustrates the mid-point method, and also incorporates site acquisition as well as building costs.

EXAMPLE 6

Problem

A site is acquired for £80 000. The estimated period required for design and tender documentation of the site development is 15 months from site acquisition, after which the building contract, estimated to be worth £550 000, can commence. The estimated contract period is $2\frac{1}{2}$ years.

Find the terminal value of the capital costs of this project at completion date.

Assume all fees and charges are included in the above figures, and that the interest rate is 8 per cent, giving factors as listed in the previous example on page 42.

Solution

The cash flow profile is indicated in Figure 5.
We proceed as follows:

Land acquisition:

$$\text{TV} = S(\text{APF}_{-n})$$
$$= 80\ 000\ (\text{APF}_{3\frac{1}{2}})$$
$$\text{APF}_3 = 1\cdot2597$$
$$\text{APF}_4 = 1\cdot3605$$

$$2\ )\overline{2\cdot6202}$$

$$\text{APF}_{3\frac{1}{2}} = 1\cdot3101$$
$$\text{APF}_4 = 1\cdot3605$$

$$2\ )\overline{2\cdot6706}$$

$$\text{APF}_{3\frac{3}{4}} = 1\cdot3353$$

$$\text{Hence}\quad 80\ 000\ (\text{APF}_{3\frac{3}{4}})$$
$$= 80\ 000 \times 1\cdot3353 \qquad = \qquad £106\ 824$$

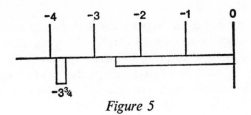

Figure 5

Building contract:

$$TV = S(APF_{-\frac{1}{4}n})$$
$$= 550\,000\,(APF_{1\frac{1}{4}})$$
$$APF_1 = 1{\cdot}0800$$
$$APF_2 = 1{\cdot}1664$$

$$2\,)\overline{2{\cdot}2464}$$

$$APF_{1\frac{1}{2}} = 1{\cdot}1232$$
$$APF_1 = 1{\cdot}0800$$

$$2\,)\overline{2{\cdot}2032}$$

$$APF_{1\frac{1}{4}} = 1{\cdot}1016$$

Hence $550\,000\,(APF_{1\frac{1}{4}})$
$$= 550\,000 \times 1{\cdot}1016 \qquad = \qquad 605\,880$$

Terminal value $\qquad = \qquad$ £712 704

In this case linear interpolation is again carried out by sub-division, this time down to quarter years.

RANKING EXERCISES

This chapter has dealt with various types of cash flow which may need to be considered when setting up a feasibility study of a construction project, and has shown how the timing of such cash flows relating to capital costs may be manipulated by compounding techniques. Before proceeding to examine the way in which these principles may be applied to problems such as leasing situations, or the setting of cost limits, it will be appropriate to conclude this chapter with some comments on feasibility studies as an aid to establishing a ranking order of projects.

Cost-in-use studies

Feasibility studies carried out at building design stage (or earlier) for the purpose of analysing the comparative economic worth of alternative design solutions are often termed cost-in-use studies. We saw in Chapter 2 how the PV method may be used to evaluate alternative window designs, and the annual equivalent method may also be found useful for this kind of analysis. Where alternative design solutions affect the income as well as the outgoings, the *net* present values of the alternatives will need to be compared. Thus a design decision which increases the lettable floor area at the expense of circulation space may increase the income of an office block, for example. To find out whether the anticipated additional income justifies the extra initial and/or maintenance cost implied by the design change requires an NPV appraisal, or its equivalent AE analysis. If there are a number of different but mutually exclusive design solutions, this becomes essentially a ranking exercise, similar in principle to the ranking of mutually exclusive capital projects at early feasibility stage of the scheme as a whole.

Present value ranking

We have seen that one advantage of the PV and AE methods over other methods of comparison is that no income need be stipulated. This makes these two methods of ranking eminently suitable for those cost-in-use studies which do not involve income. Present value with no income may be thought of as *net* present value with zero income of course, but when ranking projects (eg, design solutions) with no income considerations, one is not comparing *profitability*; one is comparing *cost* over a period of time. For the comparison to be valid, the time periods (ie, lives) of the alternatives must be identical. But when ranking alternative design elements which are part of a complete project, this will be the position in any case, since their lives will each be the complete project life. Therefore the design element with the least present value will be the cheapest.

When the question of income is considered however, the position regarding ranking order is slightly more complex, and ranking by means of present value needs more care. This is basically because the criterion now becomes one of profitability, and this quality has a number of definitions, each of which may give a different ranking order. Also, we must be careful to compare like with like when ranking. For example, projects for comparison in the feasibility study may have contract periods of differing lengths, which would mean that year 0 would occur at different times if the usual method of compounding for pre-project finance is employed. We should then be comparing present values without a common time-base, the definition of 'present' being anomalous. In such cases it is advisable to make year 0 the date of the feasibility study.

In the case of mutually compatible projects where sufficient funds are available to finance any which are profitable, the criterion of profitability is a positive NPV, projects with a negative NPV being lossmakers. However it does not follow from this that the project with the greatest NPV is necessarily the most profitable. This is because projects requiring, say, twice the capital and thus generating twice the income will have twice the NPV; but the profitability is not doubled, it remains the same.

Profitability index

Clearly a method of relating income to the amount of capital deployed is necessary for the purpose of ranking for profitability. One method has already been mentioned in Chapter 2, which is that of dividing the present value of the cash flows by the investment in each case, and ranking in order of the subsequent 'profitability indices' obtained. This has also been referred to as the benefit/cost ratio,* since it is equivalent to dividing the present value of the benefits by the present value of the costs.

If the NPV is divided by the *life* of the project, and the result expressed as a percentage of the capital outlay, we obtain a rate per cent of the average annual return on the capital, and this may be a still more meaningful index of profitability. It is not the *true* rate of return on the capital because it represents an average, the true rate being the DCF yield rate, or internal rate of return, dealt with in a later chapter.

There are two main variables in a present value comparison, namely capital and life. The purpose of a profitability index or rate of return is to take care of differences in the amount of capital outlay of the projects being compared by representing profitability as a relationship between capital and income. Differences in the lives of the projects are in a sense accounted for by the fact that, other things being equal, any additional length of life causes proportionate diminution of NPV due to the discounting of the cash flows over the additional period of time. Longer life is reflected by reduced NPV.

Payback period

Although differing lengths of life do not in general invalidate NPV ranking, marked differences between the cash flow patterns of projects with differing lives may invalidate the comparison, and may tend to affect the profitability index, especially if this is in the form of an annual rate of return. On the other hand, if the lives and net cash flows are both fairly constant, profitability will be reflected in a comparison of the payback periods of the projects.

The payback period is the time it takes for a project to earn enough money to pay back its initial capital outlay. It is not primarily used as a measure of profitability, but as an indicator of the degree of risk and liquidity involved in the project. Other things being equal, the project with the shortest payback period carries the least risk, since it involves the shortest period during which the capital is put at risk. There are circumstances where payback period may

---

*The Decision to Build, HM Stationery Office, 1970.

be a prime criterion in the selection of projects, as for example where a situation is predicted which is likely to reduce or terminate income after a certain period of time. Comparison of payback periods will indicate which projects will have recovered at least their capital by the date in question, an early payback period allowing a project sufficient time to make an adequate profit before the predicted cut-off date arrives.

Incremental yield

Where capital outlays differ, we have seen that a profitability index of some kind is necessary in order to measure return on capital. The most accurate index of profitability is the internal rate of return discussed in a later chapter. But whichever index is employed, the general principle of ranking for profitability will hold good, the higher the 'yield' (percentage of income over capital expended), the greater the profitability. It must always be remembered however that annual profit is not the same as total profit, and high early returns, if averaged over later years, will consequently tend to give a low annual rate of return to a highly profitable project. And one must also bear in mind the principle of incremental gain, which works in the following manner.

Let us consider two projects, A and B. Supposing project B costs more than project A, but brings in a higher return. Which of the two projects should be ranked the most profitable, other things being equal?

At first glance it might seem as if project B is more profitable, because the return (ie, the yield on capital) is more than that of A. However, the *extra* amount of capital required by project B, although bringing in *extra* yield, may nevertheless bring in less yield than the capital employed in project A. Hence it might be better to select project A, and employ the extra capital required by project B elsewhere.

In other words, where capital outlays differ, the yield produced by the difference (the incremental yield) should be calculated. This will also help in assessing multiple alternatives, where projects are not mutually exclusive.

Annual equivalent ranking

The annual equivalent method will give the same ranking order as the present value method in cases of projects with similar lengths of life. Where costs only are being considered, the annual equivalent is sometimes referred to as the annual capital charge (ACC method), and with income, the annual value method (AV method). It has also been referred to as the equivalent annual value method.

Where cash flows are constant annually, the AE method is convenient in that these do not need to be reduced to their present value. Where the cash flow pattern is irregular however, the PV of the cash flows needs to be found before their annual equivalent can be calculated so, other things being equal, the PV method will probably be found preferable in such cases.

Ranking methods in general

By now it will be apparent that no single ranking criterion can be described as valid under all circumstances; and when carrying out a feasibility study involving the comparative viability of alternative projects, the building economist will need to exercise care in weighing the various factors involved. Where negative cash flows only are involved, as with comparatively simple cost-in-use studies, a calculation of the present value or annual equivalent cost will probably suffice—though even in these cases the final selection may be governed by other considerations, such as the balance between initial and maintenance costs discussed earlier in this chapter.

Where income is to be taken into consideration however, ranking may involve a greater complexity of factors, and early feasibility studies of projects may require calculation of profitability yields, payback periods and incremental gain, as well as careful examination of the cash flow patterns for detection of anomalies before a decision is made on what weight should be given to net present values or annual equivalent values. Only then will the client be in possession of sufficient data on which to base his management decision.

Finally it must be emphasized that in private enterprise development and other cases where the client may be subject to the complexities of the Inland Revenue, the question of taxation must be taken into account in ranking exercises, and the question of inflation may need to be considered as well. Both taxation and inflation are dealt with separately in later chapters.

Chapter 5
Leasing decisions and cost limits

The present value and annual equivalent methods may be used for ranking of projects in order of ultimate cost or profitability. Where income is being taken into account, the present value of positive less negative cash flows gives the net present value, the project with the highest NPV ranking as the most profitable.

One must at the same time bear in mind the limitations of the PV method of comparison; schemes of differing project lives and capital outlays may not be strictly comparable on the basis of net present value only. The payback periods may need to be taken into account, and profitability indices established. In particular the internal rate of return is a criterion of profitability which is an essential ranking index for speculative development projects.

However, use of the PV and AE methods are not confined solely to straightforward ranking exercises, and the purpose of this chapter is to show some examples of how these two basic methods may be employed to carry out feasibility studies, using some of the concepts discussed in the last chapter. We have already seen how the annual equivalent method of comparison is used to calculate the total annual cost-in-use of a project, including its initial capital costs. Projects may be ranked by this method, or the AE may be used in order to compare with the alternative of renting or leasing.

LEASING DECISIONS

Given the alternative of buying or renting (leasing) over a given period, the cash flows of the two alternatives could be reduced to their present values, and these present values compared. The rent will already be expressed as an annual amount (ie, annual equivalent) however, and it will probably therefore be more convenient to calculate the AE of buying (or building), which can then be directly compared with the rent. This is often known as a lease or buy problem. The AE method, as we have seen, is sometimes known as the AV (annual value) or the ACC (annual capital charge) method. The terms 'annuity method' and 'cost-in-use method' have also been applied in this context.

Planning efficiency
The rent charged may be on the basis of so much per square metre of *net* usable floor area. This may differ from the *gross* floor area, because of the

requirement of circulation space etc, and allowance for any such difference will need to be made when comparing the cost of building with the cost of renting. The ratio between lettable area and gross area is sometimes referred to as the *planning efficiency*. The following definitions laid down by the BCIS Standard Form of Cost Analysis may be useful in this connection.

GROSS FLOOR AREA
1. Total of all enclosed spaces fulfilling the functional requirements of the building measured to the internal structural face of the enclosing walls.
2. Includes area occupied by partitions, columns, chimney breasts, internal structural or party walls, stairwells, lift wells and the like.
3. Includes lift, plant, tank rooms and the like above main roof slab.
4. Sloping surfaces such as staircases, galleries, tiered terraces and the like should be measured flat on plan.
   Note: (i) Excludes any spaces fulfilling the functional requirements of the building which are not enclosed spaces (eg, open ground floors, open covered ways and the like). These should each be shown separately.
   (ii) Excludes private balconies and private verandas which should be shown separately.

NET FLOOR AREA
Net floor area shall be measured within the structural face of the enclosing walls as 'Usable', 'Circulation' and 'Ancillary' as defined below. Areas occupied by partitions, columns, chimney breast, internal structural or party walls are excluded from these groups, and shown separately under 'Internal divisions'.

1. Usable:
   Total area of all enclosed spaces fulfilling the main functional requirements of the building (eg, office space, shop space, public house drinking area, etc).
2. Circulation:
   Total area of all enclosed spaces forming entrance halls, corridors, staircases, lift wells, connecting links and the like.
3. Ancillary:
   Total area of all enclosed spaces for lavatories, cloakrooms, kitchens, cleaners' rooms, lift, plant and tank rooms and the like, supplementary to the main function of the building.
4. Internal divisions:
   The area occupied by partitions, columns, chimney breasts, internal structural or party walls.
   Note: The sum of the areas falling in the categories defined above will equal the gross floor area.

NET HABITABLE FLOOR AREA (RESIDENTIAL BUILDINGS ONLY)

1. Total area of all enclosed spaces forming the dwelling measured within the structural internal face of the enclosing walls.
2. Includes areas occupied by partitions, columns, chimney breasts and the like.
3. Excludes all balconies, public access spaces, communal laundries, drying rooms, lift plant and tank rooms and the like.

It is emphasized that the foregoing definitions are designed for cost *analysis* purposes, and caution should therefore be used when applying them to cost *appraisal* problems to ensure that they are fully appropriate to the particular problem in hand. The term 'net floor area' for instance when used by a developer may well mean *net lettable floor area*, which may or may not include ancillary and internal divisions areas, depending on the circumstances.

The term *planning efficiency* is used in cost appraisal in connection with net gross floor area ratios; but it will be appreciated that this term is also used in a wider sense by architects and planners to denote optimum space use, and when so employed may have non-financial considerations.

Lease or buy problems

A typical example of a lease or buy situation is exemplified by the following problem.

EXAMPLE 7

Problem

A client requiring 4500 m² of usable floor space has the alternative of leasing part of an office building or leasing a site and erecting a building for his exclusive use. Show how you would evaluate these alternatives, using the data given below.

Annual rent of office building in-
cluding all rates and running costs = £16·50 per m²
Ground rent of building site   = £25 000 per annum with premium of £50 000
Building cost   = £66 per m² of gross floor area
Annual rates and running costs   = £20 000
Repair and maintenance of fabric   = £20 000 at intervals of 10 years
Replacement of service installations = £75 000 at intervals of 30 years

Terms of lease   = 80 years
Assumed rate of interest   = 5% (tables given below)

Yrs	PV factor	SF factor
5	0·7835	0·1810
10	0·6139	0·0795
15	0·4810	0·0463
20	0·3769	0·0302
25	0·2953	0·0210
30	0·2314	0·0151
40	0·1420	0·0083
50	0·0872	0·0048
60	0·0535	0·0028
70	0·0329	0·0017
80	0·0202	0·0010

Solution

The AE method of comparison is suitable for evaluating these alternatives, using the AE formulae summarized in Chapter 3 (see page 27). We find the annual equivalent of the new building project, and then compare this with the annual rent, thus:

AE of new building project:
Formulae
(1) Initial costs: $AE = CB(SF_n + i)$
(2) Annual costs: simply set down
(3) Periodic costs:
     (i) Uniform sums: $AE = C_p(\sum PVF)(SF_n + i)$
     (ii) Uniform sums and periods
          (no final payment): $AE = C_p(SF_p - SF_n)$

(1) *Initial costs*
In this case the site is leasehold and is therefore a wasting asset, the initial cost of which must be added to the building costs and treated as such. The building cost is quoted at so much per m² of *gross* floor area, but the client requires to lease 4500 m² of *usable* floor space. Hence we need to add an appropriate allowance for circulation space (including ancillary and internal divisions spaces). We proceed as follows.

	£
Leasehold premium	50 000
Building: 4500 m² @ £66	297 000
Circulation space (say) 20%	59 400
Fees (say) 10% building costs	37 125
Initial costs	£443 525

$AE = CB(SF_n + i)$

SF over 80 yrs	=	0·0010		
Interest @ 5%		0·05		
£443 525	×	0·0510	=	£22 620

(2) *Annual costs*

Ground rent	25 000
Rates and running costs	20 000

(3) *Periodic costs*

£

Maintenance every 10 yrs			20 000	

$AE = C_p(SF_p - SF_n)$

SF over 10 yrs	=	0·0795		
SF over 80 yrs	=	0·0010		
£20 000	×	0·0785	=	£1 570

Replacements every 30 yrs		75 000	

$AE = C_p(\sum PVF)(SF_n + i)$

PVF 30 yrs	=	0·2314		
PVF 60 yrs	=	0·0535		
£75 000	×	0·2849	=	£21 368
$(21\,368)(SF_n + i) = (21\,368)(0\cdot0010 + 0\cdot05)$			=	1 090

Annual equivalent of new project	=	£70 280
Annual rent of new office = 4500 m² @ £16·50	=	74 250
less		70 280
Hence annual saving from new building	=	£3 970

Note 1. The terms of the lease are here assumed not to include a full repairing clause which would require maintenance to be carried out in year 80 prior to handing over to the lessor.

Note 2. The leasehold premium figure of £50 000 has been deemed to include all site acquisition fees and charges for the purpose of this question.

Note 3. The figure of 20 per cent for cirulation space is an arbitrary one, since no design criteria are available in this instance. (No data concerning pre-project finance is available, and this has been ignored in the worked solutions given in this chapter.)

Rent fixing problems

A further aspect of leasing decisions are problems arising from the point of view of the lessor rather than the lessee. For example, a speculative developer may wish to lease or let rather than to sell outright, in which case the project appraisal will need to take account of income in the form of rent in respect of whole or part of the development. It may be necessary to calculate the minimum income necessary to sustain financial viability and then to take advice on whether such rents would be forthcoming in the area, prior to proceeding with the scheme. The following rent calculation problem illustrates this point.

EXAMPLE 8

Problem

Assume that a site is developed and sold at the market value of £340 000. What should the combined rent be if the landlord expects a return of 12 per cent on his investment over the 30 years calculated life and his annual costs are 15 per cent of the gross annual income? The years purchase for a 12 per cent return over 30 years is 8·055.

Solution

Here we know the initial cost and the discount rate (12 per cent) and are simply required to find its annual equivalent over 30 years, which, when the 15 per cent annual costs are added, will be the rent required to give a 12 per cent return.

			£	£
Initial cost			340 000	
$AE = CB(SF_n + i)$				
SF over 30 years (12%)	=	0·004147		
Interest @ 12%	=	0·12		
£340 000	×	0·124147	=	42 210
Annual costs 15% of gross	= add 3/17			7 449
Combined rent required			=	£49 659

It is interesting to note that the years purchase factor is given in the question rather than the sinking fund factor. This is because it so happens that an alternative method of calculating the answer is to divide the initial cost by the YP factor to give the annuity. Since the YP factor multiplied by an annuity gives its present value (years purchase being the present value of a pound per annum) it follows conversely that the PV divided by the YP results in the annuity, thus:

$$\text{Annuity} = \frac{\text{Present value}}{\text{YPF}}$$

$$= \frac{340\ 000}{8\cdot055}$$

$$=\quad 42\ 210$$

Add 3/17   7 449

Rent required £49 659

Both methods require only one reference to tables but the first one avoids long division, and the separation of sinking fund and interest reminds us that if the sale were freehold the site would not be a wasting asset and the landlord's return would be greater by the amount of sinking fund saved. With high interest rates however, the range of most SF tables may be exceeded, making it convenient to use the YP tables with their generally greater percentage range.

Rent fixing with periodic costs
Calculation of minimum rents will usually need to take account of periodic as well as annual costs, as illustrated by the following problem.

EXAMPLE 9

Problem

Prepare a feasibility study for a supermarket assuming that the building cost is £350,000 and the area 10,000 m². Include for professional fees 10 per cent, annual overhead management costs, ground rent and profits at £2,000 per annum. Allow for developer's profits, legal charges and contingencies, 20 per cent of building costs. Assume the expected life of the building is 60 years and the engineering services (costing £75,000) 30 years, that the annual cost for heating, lighting and cleaning is £5,000 per annum, that redecoration costs £3,000 every 5 years and that large-scale alterations may cost £20,000 every 20 years.

Calculate the annual overall minimum rent per square metre which should be obtained on this development assuming interest on capital at 7 per cent.

The following annual equivalents of an initial payment of £1 may be used.

Yrs	Rate of interest at 7%
5	0·24389
10	0·14238
15	0·10980
20	0·09439
25	0·08581
30	0·08059
60	0·07123

Solution

As with the previous example, the minimum rent is the annual equivalent of the project as a whole, the 'landlord's' profit being the discount rate of 7 per cent, plus in this case a further profit allowed for in the annual costs. The AE of the project is the minimum rent. This needs to include the developer's profit which was deemed included in the initial cost in the last example, but which requires to be calculated in this case; likewise professional fees.

Ground rent is mentioned, and the site must therefore be leasehold, no premium being stated and none payable presumably. Hence no initial cost for the land. It will be assumed in this case that the land is held under a *full repairing lease*, requiring maintenance and decorations to be carried out (fair wear and tear excepted) in the year of expiration of the lease—year n in fact— such a clause being by no means unusual in traditional leasehold practice.

It should be noted that the table given with this question is a table of *annual equivalents of an initial payment*. This is sometimes called 'the annuity a pound will purchase', and is the annual version of the monthly 'mortgage instalment tables'. It is in fact a table of sinking fund plus interest factors, from which SF + i can be read directly, which is convenient.

We proceed as follows:

AE of total cost	£
Annual costs:	
Management costs, ground rent and profits	2 000
Heating, lighting and cleaning	5 000

Initial costs:
$AE = CB(SF_n + i)$

	£	
Building cost	350 000	
Professional fees 10%	35 000	
Developer's profit, legal charges and contingencies		
= 20% of building cost	70 000	

		455 000		
SF + i over 60 yrs	×	0·07123	=	£32 410

Periodic costs:
Redecorations every 5 yrs   3 000
$AE = C_p(SF_p)$
$SF + i = 0.24389$
$\quad\ i = 0.07$

$SF_p\quad = 0.17389$	×	3 000	=	£522

Engineering services renewal
$AE = C_p(SF_p - SF_n)$
$\quad = (75\,000)\,(SF_{30} - SF_{60})$
$\quad = (75\,000)\,(0.01059 - 0.00123)$ =   £702

Alterations
$AE = C_p(SF_p - SF_n)$
$\quad = (20\,000)\,(SF_{20} - SF_{60})$
$\quad = (20\,000)\,(0.02439 - 0.00123)$ =   £463

AE of total cost	£41 097

AE of total cost divided by floor area:

$$= \frac{41\,097}{10\,000} = £4.11$$

Hence minimum rent = £4·11 per m²

Note. It has been assumed that no final payment in year n is required in the case of engineering services renewal or alterations, and because

$$SF_p - SF_n = (SF + i)_p - (SF + i)_n$$

the factors can be read straight off the table in this case, the interest cancelling out.

COST LIMITS

We have seen how minimum rents may be calculated by means of a feasibility study, using the annual equivalent method. Similar principles may be used to calculate the maximum value of the initial costs, assuming a given income, eg, to calculate the cost limits for the building contract and/or site acquisition. It is usually convenient to use the present value method for such problems, the PV of the total outgoings less the PV of the total income being the money available for land and buildings. Alternatively, if the developer wishes to sell and the market value of the developed site is known, a simple calculation will determine the initial cost limits.

We will take this last alternative first, and for an example to illustrate the calculation of site cost limits where market values are known, let us consider the following problem.

EXAMPLE 10

Problem

A developer can borrow £300 000 for investment in a site where planning permission has been granted for light industrial workshops of 4,000 m² and ancillary office accommodation of 400 m².

Assuming realistic building costs, what can the developer pay for the land if the market value of the fully developed site is estimated at £340 000 and he wants a net profit on his investment of 15 per cent?

Solution

			£
Land + building + profit	= £340 000		
but profit	= 15%		
therefore £340 000	= 115% of land + building		
hence land + building	$= \dfrac{340\,000}{115} \times 100$ =		296 000

		£	
Deduct cost of building:			
4 000 m² @ (say) £40	=	160 000	
400 m² @ (say) £50	=	20,000	
Cost of building		£180 000	180 000
Amount available for land			£116 000

The above figures are assumed to be inclusive of all fees and charges, the building cost per m² being an assumed estimate made in 1972.

Building cost limits

Where a speculative development is to be built for letting purposes, the rents obtainable may be estimated, together with the outgoings, and a present value analysis will then reveal the building cost limits. In such cases there will of course be two profit elements: (*a*) the developer's profit and (*b*) the 'landlord's' profit. The developer's profit is for entrepreneurial risk and is regarded as part of the initial costs. The landlord's profit may be usefully thought of as being contained in the discount rate. Thus, should the developer be forced to sell instead of letting, the market price will enable the developer to sell at a profit even though he has received no income from the property.

Where a scheme is divided into different classes of accommodation, the present value of the income, less the present value of the outgoings, will establish the cost limit for the total initial costs, but the individual cost limits for each class of accommodation will then need to be found by means of apportionment. Where different rents are being charged, apportionment according to income might be desirable, so that each part of the scheme is independently viable. The following question indicates the kind of problem involved in such a case, and illustrates an example of using the PV method of establishing building cost limits.

EXAMPLE 11

Problem

Prepare a feasibility study to erect a three-storey block of twelve flats, a terrace of six four-bedroom houses and a separate block of eighteen garages. It is considered that the annual rent that can be obtained for each unit is as follows:

Flats £400, houses £600, garages £100. It is estimated that the landlord's annual costs will be 20 per cent of the annual income.

The site, which is cleared and level with suitable access roads and services, is offered at £10,000.

The client requires a development profit of at least 20 per cent. What would be the building costs per square metre that could be afforded for the various categories of accommodation taking into account professional fees at 10 per cent and a net dwelling area of 75 m² and 110 m² for the flats and houses respectively?

The life of the buildings may be assumed at 60 years, the annual return to be 7 per cent giving a years purchase figure of approximately 14.

The present value of one pound over this period is 0·017 and the annual sinking fund contribution is 0·002.

Solution

We proceed as follows:
- (*a*) find PV of total income
- (*b*) find PV of total outgoings
- (*c*) deduct ancillary initial costs from the difference = money available for building
- (*d*) apportion money between various categories of accommodation.

		£
(*a*) *PV of income*		
Rent for 12 flats @ £400		4,800
Rent for 6 houses @ £600		3,600
Rent for 18 garages @ £100		1,800
Total income		£10 200
PV = C_a(YPF) = (10 200) (14)	=	142 800

(*b*) *PV of outgoings*
Outgoings = 20% of rents pa
= 20% of £10 200 = £2 040

PV = C_a(YPF) = (2 040) (14)	=	28 560
Available for initial costs		£114 240

(*c*) *Ancillary initial costs*

		£	
Developer's profit			
20% = 1/6 of 114 240	=	19 040	
Cost of land		10 000	
			29 040
Available for building			£85 200
Professional fees 10%			
= 1/11 of £85 200			7 745
Building contract cost limit			£77 455

(*d*) *Apportionment*
Income: flats £4,800, houses £3 600, garages £1 800
48 + 36 + 18 = 102

			£
Cost: flats	= $\dfrac{77\ 455}{102} \times 48 =$		36 449

$$\text{houses} = \frac{77\,455}{102} \times 36 = \qquad\qquad\qquad 27\,337$$

$$\text{garages} = \frac{77\,455}{102} \times 18 = \qquad\qquad\qquad 13\,669$$

crosscheck £77 455

Hence building costs per m²:

Flats: 12 flats @ 75 m² net
            add 20% 15 circulation
            ___
            12 flats @ 90 gross   = 1 080 m²

$$\text{Cost per m}^2 = \frac{36\,449}{1\,080} \qquad\qquad = \text{£33·75 per m}^2$$

Houses: 6 houses @ 110 m² = 660 m²

$$\text{Cost per m}^2 = \frac{27\,337}{660} \qquad\qquad = \text{£41·42 per m}^2$$

Garages: 18 garages @ (say) 15 m² = 270 m²

$$\text{Cost per m}^2 = \frac{13\,669}{270} \qquad\qquad = \text{£50·63 per m}^2$$

Note 1. The professional fees mentioned in the question are assumed to refer to QS and design fees, land acquisition charges being deemed included in the figure of £10 000.

Note 2. The percentages quoted of 20 per cent and 10 per cent for profit and fees respectively are additions to the net figures, making the gross figures 120 per cent and 110 per cent. The fractions to be deducted are therefore one-sixth and one-eleventh respectively in order to arrive at the net amounts.

Note 3. The question gives a 'net dwelling area' for the flats and houses. An arbitrary figure of 20 per cent for circulation, etc has been added to give the gross area of the flats (no design criteria being available), the net and gross areas for the houses being assumed identical for present purposes.

It might have been appropriate to cost the garages in with the flats, since they are presumably intended for the tenants of the flats, especially as no floor area is mentioned for the garages. In the above solution an estimated figure of 15 m² has been assumed and the garages apportioned separately, since the question does give garage rents and asks for costs of the 'various categories of accommodation', including presumably the accommodation for the cars.

Chapter 6
Principles of yield analysis

Consider the following problem. The estimates for two alternative designs for an office block total £2 223 000 and £2 522 000 respectively.

Both designs have a gross floor area of 22 000 square metres, and an assumed investment life of 25 years.

Given this data, how should we set about answering the following question:

'If the offices can be let for an annual rent of £22 per m² of usable area inclusive of the provision of running costs, will either design give an annual return of 8 per cent with an initial developer's profit of 20 per cent?'*

Note we are not asked to state the actual return itself, but merely to say whether it will amount to 8 per cent or not.

It might at first be thought that there is little to choose between the last two requirements, since we shall need to calculate the return in order to see whether it amounts to 8 per cent. But this is not necessarily the case, since we can easily test for 8 per cent plus or minus, whereas to pinpoint the exact percentage may not be quite so simple, depending on the data. To understand why this is so, we need first to examine what is meant by the phrase 'annual return'.

The internal rate of return

Profitability can be defined and measured in different ways. For the purpose of ranking projects in order of profitability, the 'profitability index' method (of dividing the PV of cash flows by the investment) might be a useful concept, as we saw in Chapter 2. However, if we wish to compare the profitability of a project not only with other similar projects, but with the alternative of investing the money in something entirely different (such as leaving it where it is, for example, or using it to expand production or investing it in stocks and shares) we shall need to use a yardstick of profitability of more general application. Now the universal yardstick of profitability by which we can measure the worth of the use of money is by calculating the percentage of profit which accrues by its use.

There are various methods of doing this, each giving different results. However, the method which may be said to give the 'truest' (or most generally useful) result is to calculate the amount of annual profit at compound interest on the capital left outstanding in the project at the end of each year, and to express the result as a percentage rate. This rate is known as the *internal rate of return* (IRR).

*Quoted from an RICS examination paper in Building Economics and Cost Planning.

The internal rate of return may also be defined as: 'the rate of interest which makes the present-day value of future cash flows equal in total to the present-day cost of the project'.*

In other words, to find the internal rate of return we merely select the rate of interest which will discount the net future earnings of the project to a PV equal to the initial costs. This discount rate is then the true rate of profitability of the project.

Now if we select a rate at random and find that the PV of the income is *greater* than the initial costs, we shall know the rate is too low; and vice versa. So we are now in a position to return to the problem at the beginning of this chapter and see whether the given rate of 8 per cent is high or low when we discount the income at 8 per cent and compare its present value with the initial costs in the case of each alternative project.

Before doing so, two observations arise. Firstly we are of course assuming that the words annual return in the question equate with 'internal rate of return' as defined above. Some terms in use which are synonymous with *internal rate of return* are as follows:

(1) DCF return
(2) yield rate
(3) DCF yield
(4) actuarial return
(5) interest rate of return
(6) investor's method
(7) marginal efficiency of capital.

It is reasonable to suppose that 'annual return' is yet another variant, and is not intended to denote a rate of return on capital based on methods of approximation.

Secondly, it is worth noting that the words 'present-day cost' of the project in the above IRR definition may include future *negative* cash flows discounted to their present values, as well as the initial costs, since this gives the same result as using future net positive cash flows, as will be seen later in this chapter.

To return now to the initial problem, which will be re-stated for convenience, with some additional data concerning planning efficiency and running costs.

EXAMPLE 12

Problem

The estimates for two alternative designs for an office block total (*a*) £2 223 000 and (*b*) £2 522 000.

*Dr J. M. S. Risk, 'DCF without Tears', *Chartered Secretary*, May, 1966.

Both designs have a gross floor area of 22,000 m² and an investment life of 25 years, but the ratio of lettable space to circulation areas etc are: scheme (*a*) 100:25 and scheme (*b*) 100:40.

The present value of the running costs is calculated to be: (*a*) £1 271 000 and (*b*) £997 000.

If the offices can be let for an annual rent of £22 per m² of usable area, inclusive of the provision of running costs, will either design give an annual return of 8 per cent with an initial developer's profit of 20 per cent?

Solution

For convenience, the symbol K = 1,000 is used in conjunction with the pound sign.

	Scheme (a) £K	Scheme (b) £K
Total building cost	2 223	2 522
Developer's profit 20%	445	504
Initial costs	2 668	3 026
PV of running costs	1 271	997
PV of outgoings	3 939	4 023

Income from rent:
Scheme (a)
Gross area 22 000 m²
Planning efficiency: 100:25
net area = 22 000 − 1/5
= 17 600 @ £22 = £387K pa
PV of rent @ 8% = 387 × 10·68 YPF =   4 133

Scheme (b)
Gross area 22 000 m²
Planning efficiency: 100:40
net area = 22 000 × 100/140
= 15 714 @ £22 = £346K pa
PV of rent @ 8% = 346 × 10·68 YPF =   3 695

                    +194   −328

Therefore Scheme (*a*) will yield 8%, Scheme (*b*) not.

We have discounted the income from both schemes at 8 per cent and Scheme (*a*) still shows a positive PV when the discounted income is added to the (negative) initial cost. Its profitability must therefore be greater than 8 per cent (before tax of course), as against Scheme (*b*) which must be less.

The above simple example has been used in order to introduce the reader to the concept of IRR as a yardstick of profitability. Methods of calculating the IRR or *yield rate* (a less precise but more usual term), will now be investigated.

Regular cash flow profiles

Where the cash flow 'profile' is regular, ie, comprises an initial investment followed by either (*a*) one single payment or (*b*) a series of uniform sums at uniform intervals (annual rent for example), the calculation of the yield rate is quite straightforward.

Let us first take the case of one single payment where, for instance, a developer erects a building and sells it after n years. Then (ignoring extraneous factors such as taxation, dealt with a little later in this book) the profit he makes is not a percentage based on the selling price minus the buying price (since this ignores the principle of discounted cash flow) but is the internal rate of return, or yield rate.

Now we have seen that this rate is the rate which makes the PV of future cash flows equal the present-day cost (investment). But the present value of a future sum S is given by the formula:

$$PV = \frac{S}{(1 + r)^n}$$

If the PV is now substituted for the initial investment E, we get:

$$E = \frac{S}{(1 + r)^n}$$

and r now represents the *internal rate of return*. Thus we could calculate the IRR algebraically by transformation as follows:

$$r = \sqrt[n]{\frac{S}{E}} - 1$$

where r is the yield rate. In practice there is a simpler method however, which will now be described.

Yield rate by table inspection

If instead of algebraic notation we use a table-directive formula, then $PV = S/(1 + r)^n$ becomes:

$$PV = S(PVF)$$

meaning that we simply multiply the future sum by the appropriate PV factor to find its present value. If the initial investment E is now substituted for the PV, we get:

$$E = S(PVF)$$

and by transformation:

$$PVF = \frac{E}{S}$$

or as it is usually written:

$$PVF = \frac{\text{capital}}{\text{income}}$$

This gives the PV factor of the *yield rate* (provided the income is a single future sum) which we can find in the PV tables against the appropriate year value, we can then read off the percentage rate direct.

As will be seen, the same method can be used where the income is a series of regular payments, and this method of obtaining the yield rate by means of table inspection requires very little practice to perfect. A simple example will make this clear.

EXAMPLE 13

Problem

Find the yield rate given the following data:
investment = £100K
income = £150K lump sum after 5 years
K = 1000.

Solution

$$PVF = \frac{\text{capital}}{\text{income}} = \frac{100}{150} = 0.6667$$

Now find 0·6667 in the PV table against 5 years.
From tables:

yrs	7½%	8%	8½%	9%	9½%
5	0·6966	0·6806	0·6650	0·6499	0·6352

Reading across at year 5 we find that $8\frac{1}{2}$ per cent at 0·6650 is very close indeed to 0·6667.

$$\text{Hence yield rate} = 8\tfrac{1}{2}\%$$

Yield rate with uniform earnings

If instead of a single sum we have an annuity, we merely substitute the YP factor for the PV factor when finding the yield rate by table inspection.

This is because the present value of an annual sum is PV = S(YPF), and substituting we get E = S(YPF) hence:

$$YPF = \frac{E}{S}$$

which is usually written as:

$$YPF = \frac{\text{capital}}{\text{annuity}}$$

We then proceed in the same manner as before, this time using the years purchase (present value of one pound per annum) tables instead of the PV tables.

Interpolation between rates

When using the table inspection method it may happen that the calculated value falls between two adjacent factors in the tables, in which case interpolation will be called for, unless the value is very close to one of the factors. Strictly speaking the table factors do not form a straight-line relationship, but for short lives this may be ignored, and even for longer lives and higher percentages the relationship is almost straight-line between adjacent percentage integers. So in practice it is usual to regard straight-line interpolation as quite valid for this present purpose, especially when one considers that the cash flows themselves are normally estimated figures only.

A useful formula for straight-line interpolation is given by:

$$f = \frac{H - G}{H - L}$$

where f = decimal fraction to add to lower rate
      H = higher factor in tables
      L = lower factor in tables
      G = given factor (calculated)

EXAMPLE 14

Problem

Find the yield rate given the following data:
investment = £100K
income = £30K per annum
life of project = 5 years
K = 1000.

Solution

$$YPF = \frac{\text{capital}}{\text{annuity}} = \frac{100}{30} = 3 \cdot 333$$

Now find 3·333 in the YP table against 5 years.
From tables:

yrs	14%	15%	16%	17%
5	3·433	3·352	3·274	3·199

Reading across at year 5 we find that 3·333 falls in between 15 per cent and 16 per cent.
Interpolation:

$$f = \frac{H - G}{H - L}$$

$$= \frac{3 \cdot 352 - 3 \cdot 333}{3 \cdot 352 - 3 \cdot 274}$$

$$= 0 \cdot 24$$

Add 0·24 to lower rate of 15 per cent
Yield rate = 15·24%

Irregular cash flow profiles

If we regard the initial investment as a negative cash flow and the future pattern of income as positive cash flows, we can say that the yield rate can be found by table-inspection (and hence by algebraic formula) when income is represented by (*a*) a single positive cash flow, or (*b*) a series of uniform positive cash flows.

Where cash flows are represented by any other pattern however, the general equation for finding the yield rate is as follows:

$$E = \sum \frac{S}{(1 + r)^n}$$

or, if S is a negative cash flow:

$$E + \sum \frac{S}{(1 + r)^n} = 0$$

where E = the investment
     S = a future negative cash flow
     r = the yield rate
     n = the year in which each S occurs

In the above equation $\sum \dfrac{S}{(1 + r)^n}$ is said to represent a Financial Model

(or mathematical model) M of the project, where:

$$E + M = 0$$

Now the reason for introducing financial model M to the reader in this way is not to confound him with mathematical jargon, but to indicate why this particular general equation is not soluable by ordinary algebraic means. This is because, since the cash flow pattern under discussion is irregular (not a uniform series), S is a variable quantity, so that we cannot solve for r by means of a simple formula.

In fact our financial model of a development project will almost certainly contain negative as well as positive cash flows: annual and periodic costs as well as annual income. And when we take taxation into account later on, there will also be tax payments and investment allowances to consider, making the financial model more complex. This is when we shall find a computer very useful in order to save time; but ordinary manual methods are easy to learn, and it is now proposed to deal with the method of finding the yield rate of irregular cash flows by means of manual trial discounting procedures. First however it might be helpful to recap a little in order to clarify further the basic definitions in relation to yield analysis (ie, finding the yield rate).

The student may perhaps find it convenient to skim through these yield rate definitions on first reading, and return to them later, after reading the remainder of the chapter.

Yield rate definitions
The yield rate has been defined as the rate of return which makes the PV of

future cash flows equal to the initial investment; or, to return to the discount notation used earlier in this book, the yield rate is r in the following equation:

$$\left| E_0 \right| = \sum_r^0 \left| S \right| \qquad \dots \dots (1)$$

where E is the investment in year 0 and S is a cash flow discounted to year 0 at the rate r.

Now in the above, S represents a net positive cash flow. But since some future cash flows will be negative, it may well be more convenient to deal with these separately, the equation becoming:

$$\sum_r^0 \left| P \right| = \sum_r^0 \left| N \right| \qquad \dots \dots (2)$$

where P and N are positive and negative cash flows respectively, the investment now being treated as a negative cash flow.

This provides for the investment occurring other than in year 0. If it does occur in year 0, it may be separated from the other cash flows thus:

$$\left| E_0 \right| = \sum_r^0 \left| P \right| - \sum_r^0 \left| N \right| \qquad \dots \dots (3)$$

the rate r still being the yield rate.

From the foregoing it will be apparent that there are at least three valid definitions of the yield rate, corresponding to the three discount notation equations above: that is, the rate which makes:

(1) PV of future net cash flows
    = investment
(2) PV of positive cash flows
    = PV of negative cash flows
(3) NPV of positive and negative cash flows
    = investment

These three definitions are three different ways of saying the same thing. Or, to put it another way, we could quote from Merrett & Sykes* and define the yield rate as 'the true annual rate of return on the capital outstanding in the investment'.

Trial discounting procedures

Since the discount rate cannot be expressed algebraically as a function of the cash flow and the investment, in the case of irregular cash flow profiles, trial discounting procedures will need to be carried out where cash flows of

*Capital Budgeting and Company Finance, Longman, 1966.

differing sums and periods are encountered. The principle involved is to discount the cash flows at trial rates until a rate is chosen such that their PV is equal to the initial costs; this rate is then the yield rate (see Figure 6). We have seen above, however, that the yield rate is also the rate which makes the PV of positive cash flows equal to the PV of negative cash flows, or:

$$\sum_r {}^0 \left| N \right| = \sum_r {}^0 \left| P \right|$$

alternatively:

$$N(PVF) = P(PVF)$$

where P and N are the sum of the negative and positive cash flows respectively. Now if we divide both sides by P(PVF) we obtain:

$$\frac{N(PVF)}{P(PVF)} = 1$$

which is the key to the following trial discounting technique because it tells us that the yield rate is that which discounts the cash flows such that *the PV of negative cash flows over the PV of positive cash flows equals unity.*

This knowledge can now be used to enable us to home in on the yield rate with very few trial runs by taking rates which discount to results which fall either side of unity, and interpolating the results by graphic or other means.

Search reduction formula

If we intend to discount all the cash flows at a number of trial rates with a view to straddling the target of unity, in the manner suggested above, it will be highly desirable to first narrow the field of fire by estimating the position of the target, in order to avoid wasted trials which can be very time-consuming with complex projects. This is achieved by finding a *target rate* by means of a suitable search reduction formula, such as:

$$YPF_t = \frac{E \times L}{\sum CF}$$

where YPF_t = YPF of the target rate

E   = investment
L   = life of project
CF   = cash flows

This formula gives the YPF of the target rate, from which the rate itself can be found by inspection of the YP table. The accuracy of this formula will depend on the degree of irregularity of the actual cash flow. With a little practice it is easy to estimate from the cash flow pattern on which side of the target rate the actual yield rate will fall.

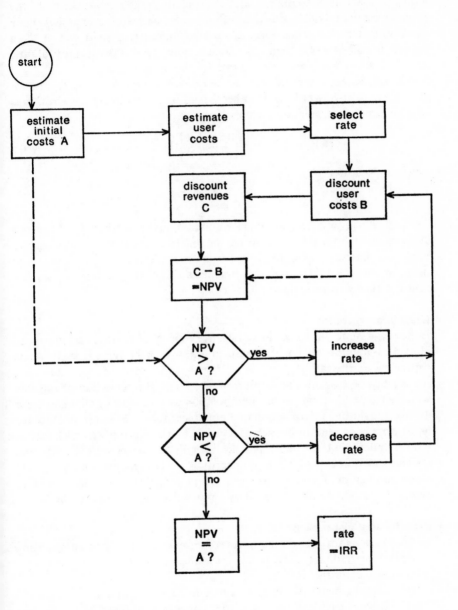

Figure 6

Yield rate interpolation

Having calculated a target rate, and straddled this rate by discounting the cash flows at rates on either side of the target, we then divide the PV of the negative by the PV of the positive cash flows for each trial rate and examine the resultant ratios in the form of decimal numbers. Should one of them happen to come to 1·00, then unity is represented by this particular trial rate, and it therefore becomes the yield rate for the project, *qed*.

As likely as not however, none of the ratios will actually be unity, and we then select the two which lie on either side of unity and interpolate by means of a yield rate interpolation formula such as:

$$\text{IRR} = \text{L}\% + \left[\frac{1\cdot0 - \text{LR}}{\text{HR} - \text{LR}}\right](\text{H}\% - \text{L}\%)$$

where L = lower
      H = higher
      R = ratio

This formula gives a straight-line interpolation, which is generally considered accurate enough for this purpose, having regard to the fact that although we might calculate the yield rate to two or more decimal places, cash flows are based on estimated data so that in practice an accuracy greater than one per cent is unlikely to be realised in any case.

Graphic interpolation

If the ratios representing the PV of negative over PV of positive cash flows are plotted on a graph, they will be seen to follow a slight curve (the slightness depending on the ratios). If a line is drawn on the graph to represent unity, the IRR can be read off the graph from the point of intersection of this line with the curve. By using graphic interpolation we theoretically eliminate error due to straight-line interpolation of a non-linear function; but in practice the linear error may tend to be merely replaced by the plotting error. One must bear in mind that for most practical conditions of percentage, life and closeness of ratios, the degree of linearity is fairly high, and the above yield rate interpolation formula has been found to collate reasonably well in practical use with results obtained by computer using iterative methods.

Rules for trial discounting

To summarise thus far, the basic rules for manual trial discounting, using numerical interpolation may be stated as follows:

(1)   calculate target rate
(2)   discount each cash outflow at trial rate and total these
(3)   discount each cash inflow at trial rate and total these
(4)   divide total (2) by total (3) = decimal ratio
(5)   repeat (2) to (4) for each trial rate
(6)   select the two ratios on either side of unity
(7)   interpolate for unity = IRR.

EXAMPLE 15

Problem

Find the yield rate given the following data:

investment	= £100K
income	= £30K per annum
annual running costs	= £10K
periodic maintenance: redecorating every 5 years	= £10K
life of project	= 10 years
where K	= 1000.

Assume full repairing lease.

Solution

The periodic maintenance costs cause this project to have an irregular cash flow pattern. Hence the yield rate cannot be found by simple table-inspection methods, and trial discounting is called for, as follows:

Calculation of target rate

Sum of cash flows:		£K	£K
income	10 × £30K		300
less running costs	10 × £10K	100	
maintenance	2 × £10K	20	120
	$\Sigma CF =$		180

$$YPF_t = \frac{E \times L}{\Sigma CF} = \frac{100 \times 10}{180} = 5 \cdot 556$$

Now find 5·556 in the YP table against 10 years.
From tables:

yrs	11%	12%	13%	14%
10	5·889	5·650	5·426	5·216

Reading across at year 10 we find that 5·556 falls between 12 per cent and 13 per cent, (say) 12½ per cent.

Hence target rate = 12½%

Select rates to straddle the target of 12½ per cent. Say 10 per cent and 15 per cent. Trial discounting at 10 per cent and 15 per cent now proceeds as follows.

Cash flow	10% factor	PV £K	15% factor	PV £K
Outflow				
Investment yr 0	1	100·00	1	100·00
Running costs £10K pa yrs 1–10	6·145	61·45	5·019	50·19
Maintenance £10K yr 5	0·621	6·21	0·497	4·97
£10K yr 10	0·386	3·86	0·247	2·47
Cash outflow		171·52		157·63
Inflow				
Income £30K pa yrs 1–10	6·145	184·35	5·019	150·57
Ratio		171·52		157·63
		———		———
		184·35		150·57
	=	0·93		1·05

Interpolation

$$\text{IRR} = L\% + \left[\frac{1 \cdot 0 - LR}{HR - LR}\right](H\% - L\%)$$

$$= 10\% + \frac{1 \cdot 0 - 0 \cdot 93}{1 \cdot 05 - 0 \cdot 93} \times 5$$

$$= 10\% + 2 \cdot 92$$

$$= 12 \cdot 92\% = \text{(say) } 13\%$$

Therefore yield rate $= 13\%$

Note. In calculating the target rate the sum of the *net* cash flows is found, negative cash flows being deducted from positive. It will not be necessary to interpolate between rates using the formula when finding the target rate from the YP table, as interpolation by inspection is sufficient for this purpose.

Chapter 7
Company taxation

The examples of investment appraisal given in this book have so far ignored the incidence of taxation. It will be evident however that when the developer is subject to assessment by the Inland Revenue, taxation will have a significant effect upon the cash flows. Indeed taxation may in some cases have the effect of turning an apparently profitable project into a loss-maker, or affecting the ranking order of projects owing to its differential application. It is essential therefore to take the full effect of taxation into account when appraising projects which are subject to it, and this chapter will attempt to lay down the principles involved in adjusting cash flows for taxation. This will be done by using the present-day United Kingdom system of taxation as an example, and employing methods of adjustment suitable for incorporation in construction project appraisals by the building economist.

First a note of caution. Both the principles of taxation and the rate of tax itself are subject to periodic changes over the years, and it is stressed that before embarking on an actual appraisal involving taxation, the appraiser must acquaint himself with the current tax situation applicable to the project in hand.

It is emphasised that the tax formulae given in this book relate only to the situation existing at time of writing, and that the tax and allowance rates used in the examples have been selected for the purpose of illustrating the general techniques involved, and are not necessarily intended to represent actual prevailing rates.

In spite of constant detailed changes imposed by government however, the broad principles of incorporating the incidence of tax charges, and writing-down allowances, balancing charges, etc, in the DCF calculations remain basically the same; and the reader will find that once these principles and their nomenclature have been grasped, it is not difficult to make any necessary adjustments to the system to bring it into line with subsequent changes in taxation.

Corporation tax

A client who initiates building development will normally do so not as a private individual but as a company.

We are not therefore concerned on the whole with the income tax paid by individual persons, but with the tax paid by companies. The Finance Act of 1965 changed the basis of company taxation and introduced *Corporation tax*, which can be thought of as an amalgamation of income tax, profits tax, and capital gains tax. Corporation tax is payable by companies, unincorporated associations, building societies and nationalised industries, but not by local authorities.

Corporation tax is paid on income, but relief is given against certain expenses which are deductible, such as repairs and maintenance. Capital improvements to premises are not deductible (capital being understood as bringing into existence an advantage), nor is capital expenditure on new buildings.

Capital allowances

Although capital expenditure on new buildings is not deductible, relief is given in the form of capital allowances for certain classes of new buildings. At time of writing these include industrial buildings, agricultural buildings, and scientific research buildings. Industrial buildings include factories, some warehouses, power-stations, waterworks, docks, bridges and tunnels. Excluded are shops, showrooms, houses, hotels or offices (except drawing-offices in factories). An industrial building may contain up to 10 per cent 'non-industrial' accommodation.

The cost of the land on which the building stands is *not* allowable, but site clearance and preparation are allowable. Plant and machinery for use in services and manufacturing is also allowable, separately from the building.

Depreciation

Capital allowances are best thought of as taxation allowances against depreciation. Depreciation is the amount set aside (usually annually) in a company's books to replace an asset when it wears out. In the words of Page and Canaway* depreciation is 'a proportion of the original cost to be debited annually as a current operating expense in the profit and loss account'.

Hence the sum of money set aside annually for depreciation in the company's books is not part of the company's profit, because it is being set aside to replace capital. But this fact is disregarded for basic tax purposes, and tax is levied on all income including that set aside for depreciation.†

The purpose of capital allowances is to allow for depreciation in certain instances and by certain amounts, regardless of the actual amounts set aside in the company's books. Thus the methods by which the Inland Revenue calculates depreciation for tax purposes may well be different from the way the company calculates the same depreciation for book purposes. One way of allowing for depreciation would be to have the asset valued annually, but with fixed assets it is more usual to calculate the depreciation by estimating the asset's life and residual value and then selecting a formula for 'writing down' the value over the life of the asset. The following is a brief summary of four such methods of calculating depreciation.

Finance for Management, Heinemann, 1966.
†Capital gains are also included in the computation, but not franked investment income.

(1) *Straight line.* This method depreciates the asset by the same *amount* each year, by means of the formula:

$$D = \frac{E - R}{L}$$

where D = annual depreciation
  E = investment (initial cost)
  R = residual value
  L = life of asset

The amounts for annual depreciation calculated by this method produce a straight line when they are plotted on a graph of money against time; hence the name.

(2) *Declining balance.* (Alternatively 'reducing balance', 'diminishing balance', 'constant percentage method', 'Matheson formula'.) This method depreciates the asset by the same *percentage* each year, by means of the formula:

$$D\% = \left[1 - \sqrt[n]{\frac{R}{E}}\right] \times 100$$

where D% = percentage of written-down value to be deducted annually
  n = life in years

The amounts for annual depreciation by this method produce a curve when plotted on the graph, giving *high-early* depreciation which never reaches zero value.

(3) *Sum of digits.* (Alternatively 'sum of integers', 'sum of years digits'.) This method gives high-early straight-line depreciation to zero value, by means of the formula:

$$D = (E - R)\left[\frac{2(n - A + 1)}{n(n + 1)}\right]$$

where D = amount of depreciation for a given year
  A = number of the year for which D is required

(4) *Sinking fund depreciation.* This method provides for a sinking fund to replace the asset, the ASF to replace one pound at the end of n years being:

$$\frac{r}{(1 + r)^n - 1}$$

This method gives low-early depreciation.

Initial and writing-down allowances
Where capital allowances for depreciation are given against taxation they may be in the form of:

(*a*) an allowance in the first year
(*b*) an annual allowance over a period or
(*c*) a combination of both.

At the time of writing for example scientific research buildings carry 100 per cent allowance in the first year. But new industrial buildings carry an allowance in the first year of 40 per cent and an annual allowance of 4 per cent starting in year one. The 40 per cent in the first year is termed an *initial* allowance, and the annual 4 per cent a *writing-down* allowance.

Where it is not able to take advantage of a full 100 per cent initial allowance, owing to insufficient taxable income against which to offset the allowance, the company may be allowed to choose instead some other method of calculating its depreciation allowance. This is known as free depreciation.

In order to take full advantage of any initial or writing-down allowances the developer must have sufficient taxable income against which to offset these allowances. Income from sources other than the project attracting the allowances can be counted for this purpose. However, if capital allowances exceed the profits of the year to which they relate, they may be carried forward and set against future profits, or in certain cases be carried back and set against profits in preceding years.

Writing-down allowances may be straight-line (as in the case of industrial buildings) or reducing-balance (as for machinery and plant prior to October 1970) or calculated by any other method laid down by the government from time to time. Capital allowances against taxation are currently (1973) as follows.

	Initial allowance	*Writing-down allowance*
	%	%
Industrial buildings	40	4
Agricultural buildings	nil	10
Farm houses (one-third)	nil	10
Scientific research buildings	100	—
Plant and machinery	100	—

In the case of farm houses only one-third of the expenditure qualifies for the allowance. Where the initial allowance is 100 per cent it is sometimes referred to as a 'first-year' allowance, to denote that no further writing-down allowance is applicable. The first-year allowance may be reduced at the taxpayer's request, and a writing-down allowance claimed in subsequent years.

Investment grants

The term 'investment incentives' is sometimes used to describe tax concessions such as capital allowances. This term also includes any incentives by way of cash grants which may be given by the government from time to time in order to encourage building or other development in certain areas of the country. Such cash grants to encourage capital investment are known as 'investment grants', and form part of the cash flows, as do taxation allowances. Since such questions may arise as whether or not the developer can obtain a tax allowance in respect of the grant, it is convenient to regard investment grants as being part of the corporation tax field of study; though a cash grant is different in principle from a tax allowance since it is of immediate benefit to firms making a loss and thus unable to benefit from a tax allowance.

The Industrial Development Act 1966 introduced certain 'development areas', ie, parts of the country attracting investment grants for certain types of building development etc. In 1971 the government announced new 'special development areas', and at present time of writing the areas attracting investment grants ('regional development grants') are collectively known as 'assisted areas'. The assisted areas currently comprise:

(*a*) special development areas
(*b*) development areas
(*c*) intermediate areas
(*d*) derelict land clearance areas
(*e*) towns where development area benefits are available, and
(*f*) towns where special development area benefits are available.

Regional development grants are obtained by application to one of the Department of Trade and Industry Regional Development Grant Offices, the rates of grant being currently (1973) as follows.

	Plant, machinery and mining works %	*Industrial buildings* %
Special areas	22	22
Development areas	20	20
Intermediate areas	nil	20
Derelict areas (for 2 years)	nil	20

The eligible cost will normally include site preparation but *not* the cost of the site; and adaptations of existing buildings qualify for grant. The grants are in effect tax-free. Grants in derelict land clearance areas are to be available for a limited period of only two years commencing from 22 March 1972.

It should be noted that where a regional development grant is at present available under this scheme, its receipt does not affect capital allowances against taxation. In other words, when grants are paid, 100 per cent of the cost of building (including grant) is regarded as available for depreciation for tax purposes. This makes grants worth more than their face value. This principle only applies to regional development grants however. Any other grant or subsidy from a government, public or local authority must be deducted in arriving at the total amount of expenditure which qualifies for an allowance.

Like initial and writing-down allowances, investment grants are subject to alteration or cancellation by government from time to time.

Balancing adjustments

Where an industrial building is sold or demolished an adjustment is made to bring the total of the writing-down allowance up or down to the net cost of the building to the taxpayer. If the written-down value is less than the sale proceeds a *balancing charge* is made to cover the difference. If the written-down value exceeds the sale proceeds (residual value) however, a further allowance, known as a *balancing allowance*, is made to allow for the difference. The operation of balancing adjustments is best clarified by giving a simple example showing also the effect of an initial and writing-down allowance.

The following example shows the initial allowance (IA) and writing-down allowance (WDA) amounts in respect of an industrial building costing £100 000, with a 40 per cent IA and a 4 per cent (straight-line) WDA.

Columns (*a*) and (*b*) show alternative effects of the balancing adjustment, depending on whether the building is sold for more or less than its written-down value (WDV) at the end of 5 years when it is sold.

Note that the WDV in year 1 is the initial cost less both the initial allowance and the first year's writing-down allowance of 4 per cent.

Yr				(*a*) £K		(*b*) £K
0		cost	=	100		100
			£K			
	IA @ 40%		40			
	WDA @ 4%		4	44		44
				———		—
1		WDV	=	56		56
	WDA @ 4% of cost			4		4
				—		—
2				52		52
				4		4
				—		—
3				48		48
				4		4
				—		—
4				44		44
				4		4
				—		—
5				40		40
		sold for		50	sold for	20
				—		—
	balancing charge			£10K	balancing allowance	£20K

Column (*a*) shows a balancing charge of £10K and column (*b*) a balancing allowance of £20K. Both figures require multiplying by the tax rate in order to calculate the cash flow represented by the balancing charge or allowance. A balancing charge can be thought of as representing a negative cash flow to the taxpayer and a balancing allowance (like the initial and writing-down allowances) may be regarded as a positive cash flow, ie, money gained to offset against tax payments.

Limitations on balancing charges

Although a balancing charge is made to cover the difference between the written-down value and the residual value, this does not apply to a case where this difference is greater than the allowances which have actually been received, when the charge is limited to the total allowances received. The allowances received amount to the cost minus the final WDV: £100K minus £40K = £60K in the above example.

Hence the asset requires to be re-sold at more than its original cost before the limit applies. When this situation occurs, a capital gain arises, which is discussed in the next chapter.

Since depreciation allowances apply to the building only and not to the land (the re-sale value of which, after apportionment, is deducted in arriving at the residual value), the chances of the residual value being greater than the initial cost are, even in times of inflation, somewhat reduced.

There is also a time limit on balancing charges, which applies also to balancing allowances. No balancing adjustment is made by reason of any event occurring more than 25 years after the building was first used (the time limit in the case of expenditure incurred on or before 5 November 1962 being 50 years).

Taxation cash flows

One way of allowing for taxation in a DCF analysis would be to calculate the cash flows for each year net of tax, and this seems to be the method normally adopted by management accountants. However, in the case of construction projects, with their relatively long lives, this method is somewhat laborious, often requiring many columns to arrive at each year's net-of-tax cash flow.

If instead of thinking in terms of annual cash flows we continue to think in terms of the present value of each type of cost or revenue (as in the last chapter for instance), we shall find that the format for trial discounting is somewhat simplified. We shall therefore not make use of the annual cash flow (horizontal) method, but continue to use the PV of costs (vertical) method. Thus it will be seen that we need to think of tax payments as an annual cost (like, for example, running costs) and of tax allowances as income, ie, positive cash flows. All we then require is some simple formulae for taxation and allowances similar to those previously used for running and periodic costs etc, so that we may correctly establish the PV of tax and allowance cash

7

flow profiles each in one operation. This is the method it is now proposed to examine.

Firstly it will be apparent that the tax payments themselves, being a function of the annual income (rent) can be regarded normally as an annual cost, dealt with by means of the YP table (with a suitable adjustment for tax lag, as will be seen later). Secondly, single sums, such as the initial allowance, will either occur in year 0 or can be dealt with by the PV table.

Items such as tax allowance in respect of allowable expenses (eg, maintenance costs) will also require adjustment, as will writing-down allowances and balancing adjustments. The writing-down allowance will be a regular annual cash flow, but the balancing allowance will require to be calculated (where applicable), as will the period over which the writing-down allowance will run. This may be done as follows.

Calculation of the asset life

To arrive at the writing-down period (and hence the written-down value, where a balancing adjustment is required prior to the end of this period) we can make use of the following formula:

$$\text{asset life} = \frac{100 - \text{IA}\%}{\text{WDA}\%}$$

where asset life = the writing-down period
IA = initial allowance
WDA = writing-down allowance

Thus, if the IA is 40 per cent and the WDA is 4 per cent, then (substituting):

$$\text{asset life} = \frac{100 - 40}{4} = \frac{60}{4} = 15 \text{ years}$$

In this case the asset would be written off over 15 years, when its written-down value would then be zero. In other words the WDA could be represented as an annual income over the first 15 years of the project (assuming no allowance for tax lag).

Calculation of the written-down value

In the above example the WDV after 15 years is nought. But if the project is sold before this, we need to calculate its WDV at the time of selling, in order to establish whether there should be a balancing charge or allowance, and if so how much.

If the project life exceeds the asset life, as in the above case, then clearly:

$$\text{WDV} = 0$$

But where the asset life exceeds the project life, the WDV is as follows:

$$\text{WDV} = \text{E} - [(\text{IA} \times \text{E}) + n(\text{WDA} \times \text{E})]$$

where E = investment (cost of building)
   n = project life
  IA = initial allowance as a decimal fraction of E
 WDA = writing-down allowance as a decimal fraction of E

Let us suppose in the above example the project life had been only 5 years. With a calculated asset life of 15 years, the asset life now exceeds the project life and therefore, assuming a £100K investment:

$$\begin{aligned}
\text{WDV} &= E - [(IA \times E) + n(WDA \times E)] \\
&= 100 - [(0{\cdot}40 \times 100) + 5(0{\cdot}04 \times 100)] \\
&= 100 - (40 + 20) \\
&= \text{£40K written-down value}
\end{aligned}$$

Calculating the balancing charge/allowance

Having calculated the WDV it will be necessary to establish the *residual value* before we can arrive at the final balancing adjustment. The residual value is the disposal price from selling or otherwise disposing of the building, and thus ending the taxable income from the property. When this residual value is estimated it must not be forgotten that it does not include the value of the land, which was excluded from the capital cost of the project when calculating the depreciation allowances in the first place. If the land and buildings are disposed of together, as may well be the case, the Inland Revenue will do a notional apportionment to arrive at the residual value of the building only. When this has been done as necessary, the formula for calculating the final balancing charge or allowance is then simply:

$$\text{BA} = \text{WDV} - \text{RV}$$

where BA = balancing adjustment figure (allowance if positive, charge if negative)*
  RV = residual value

Tax lag

Mention has been made of tax lag, which affects both tax payments and allowances, and which comes into operation in the following manner.

Tax lag is the difference between the time a taxation cash flow is received and the time the tax is actually paid. Corporation tax is normally due nine months after the end of the *accounting period* (twelve-month period forming the 'basis of assessment'). But in the case of existing companies formed prior to 1965, if the interval between the basis period for 1965/6 and 1 January 1966 was longer than nine months, that interval is allowed for corporation tax purposes instead of nine months. This means that tax lag can vary from nine to perhaps twenty-one months depending on the individual situation of the company concerned. In practice we need to bear in mind the extent to

---

*Subject to balancing adjustment limitations, described above.

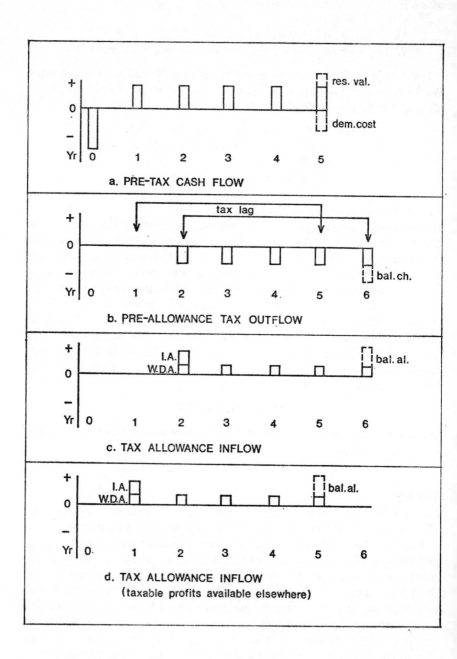

Figure 7

which the fiction of year-end discounting is resorted to in the discounting procedures and assess the appropriate tax lag allowance in the case of each individual project, after suitable consultation with the accountant responsible for the company's tax affairs.

Allowance for lag will need to be applied equally to tax allowances as well as to tax payments, since a tax allowance cannot be taken advantage of until the tax is actually paid. However, it must not be forgotten that where taxable profits are available from elsewhere within the company (other than from the project under consideration) tax allowances can be offset against these, in which case there will be no effective allowance lag as far as the project is concerned.

This situation is illustrated in Figure 7, which shows simplified cash flow profiles in respect of a five-year project subject to corporation tax and allowances. Figure 7 (*a*) shows the investment in year 0, followed by income payments in the following years, with a possible residual value and/or demolition cost cash flow in year 5. Figure 7 (*b*) shows the resultant tax payment cash flows and possible balancing charge, lagged one year; while (*c*) gives the corresponding tax allowance cash flows for initial and writing-down allowances, together with a possible balancing allowance. The effect on the allowances if taxable profits are available elsewhere is illustrated in (*d*), where allowance lag is seen to be no longer applicable.

Tax lag discount factors

In the case of single tax payments (or single 'receipts' in the form of an initial allowance, for example) the adjustment for tax lag is made in the DCF analysis by simply using the actual year of the 'cash flow' when discounting, instead of the notional 'unlagged' year. Thus in the case of an initial allowance lagged by one year, simply discount from year 2 instead of year 1 when finding the PV of the allowance.

If an annuity is concerned however, as in the case of annual tax payments or an annual writing-down allowance, it will be necessary to 'lag' the YP table. The YP table gives the present value of one pound per annum *starting from year one*. But where tax lag occurs, the annuity does not in fact start in year one, but at some time in the future, depending on the amount of lag. The present value of an annuity starting later than in year one is given by the following formula:

$$DF = (YPF_n)(PVF_L)$$

where DF = required discount factor
    n = life of annuity
    L = lag period

In other words, the discount factor giving the present value of a *future* annuity is its YP factor multiplied by the PV factor of the number of years the annuity is lagged.

Tax-free outgoings

In addition to capital allowances, certain other expenses may be allowed against corporation tax, like maintenance and business running costs (but not expenses involving 'capital' improvement). When tax payments are treated as positive cash flows and allowances as negative cash flows, it is necessary to account for the allowances in respect of maintenance and other costs by treating them as further positive cash flows; and this can be done conveniently by regarding them as reductions of the (negative) maintenance costs, which are adjusted accordingly, prior to entry as cash flows on the DCF analysis, by means of the following formula:

$$ACF = M[100\% - (T\% \times PVF_L)]$$

where ACF = adjusted cash flow
     M   = maintenance or other charge allowable against tax
     $T\%$ = tax rate
     PVF_L = PV factor of the tax lag period

Conclusions

We have seen in this chapter the ways in which the cash flows of a development project may be affected by the incidence of corporation tax and allowances, and methods have been suggested whereby the effect of tax payments, initial and writing-down allowances, balancing adjustments and tax-free outgoings may be built into a DCF analysis by the use of simple formulae. This will be illustrated with examples in the next chapter. But it would be wrong to conclude this chapter without once again stressing the need to examine carefully the current taxation situation, as it applies to the individual project in hand, before attempting to take account of taxation for a feasibility study of any kind.

Finally, it will also be appreciated that in dealing with taxation in this book it is assumed that (*a*) the developer is subject to corporation tax; (*b*) he is carrying on business in such a way as to be eligible for tax relief in respect of outgoings connected with the building; and (*c*) the project involves the type of building against which such allowances may be obtained. It will be evident also that we are looking at the problem from the point of view of the development company, and not from the point of view of its shareholders, the tax situation and profitability position of which is by no means the same, but a different problem altogether, outside the present scope of this book.

Chapter 8
DCF with corporation tax

Before proceeding with our first example of a feasibility study incorporating taxation, it will be expedient to recap a little and summarise the tax situation discussed in the last chapter, and its effect on the cash flows.

(*a*) *Tax payments.* These are treated as negative cash flows, being a percentage of the annual income which is treated as an annual outgoing, the percentage being the tax rate. The tax cash flow profile needs to be lagged by means of an adjustment to the discount factor, obtained by the formula:

$$DF = (YPF_n) (PVF_L)$$

which multiplies the YP factor of the tax annuity by the PV factor of the lag period.

(*b*) *Initial allowance.* This is treated as a single positive cash flow: a percentage of the 'cost of building' at the tax rate. It is lagged if no profits are available elsewhere.

(*c*) *Writing-down allowance.* This is treated as a positive annuity cash flow during the 'asset life'. The asset life is calculated by:

$$\text{asset life} = \frac{100 - IA\%}{WDA\%}$$

But if this exceeds the project life, the life of the WDA annuity is the project life. It is lagged if no profits are available elsewhere.

(*d*) *Balancing adjustment.* Estimate residual value and then calculate written-down value. If project life exceeds asset life:

$$WDV = 0$$

If asset life exceeds project life:

$$WDV = E[(IA \times E) + n(WDA \times E)]$$

where E is the cost of building, n the project life, and IA and WDA are expressed as a decimal fraction of E.

The balancing adjustment is then found by:

$$BA = WDV - RV$$

the balancing adjustment figure being an allowance if positive, charge if negative (subject to the limitations mentioned in Chapter 7). Treat as single cash flow at tax rate and lag if no profits available elsewhere.

(*e*) *Tax-free outgoings.* Adjust the negative cash flows of these by the tax formula:

$$ACF = M[100\% - (T\% \times PVF_L)]$$

where M is any charge allowable as a tax-free expense.

In the examples which follow it will be assumed that no profits are available elsewhere. In general, the examples have been simplified in order to demonstrate the basic technique, the term 'capital investment' denoting the cost of building including quantity surveyor's and design fees which are considered as a single cash flow in year 0. In such cases 'pre-project finance' has been ignored for the sake of simplicity, as has the cost of land (together with some other ancillary factors dealt with later on).

NPV with tax and allowances
Let us take a simple example to start with, assuming that outgoings such as running and maintenance costs are paid by the tenant, and demolition costs ignored.

EXAMPLE 16

Problem

Calculate the net present value of an investment project allowing for corporation tax at the rate of 40 per cent given the following data:

Capital investment   = £200K
initial allowance   = 40 per cent
writing-down allowance = 4 per cent
income from rents   = £40K pa

Assume a life of 20 years, after which the building will be demolished with no residual value. Allow for tax lag of one year and a discount rate of 12 per cent.

Solution

Cash flow	Discount factor	DCF £
Capital investment Yr 0	1	$-200\,000$
Initial allowance 40% of £200K @ 40% tax $= (0.40)(200)(0.40)$ $= £32K$ in yr 2	0.7972	$+25\,510$
WD allowance 4% of £200K @ 40% tax $= (0.04)(200)(0.40)$ $= £3.2K$ $AL = \dfrac{100 - IA\%}{WDA\%}$ $= \dfrac{100 - 40}{4} = \dfrac{60}{4}$ $= 15$ yrs 1 yr tax lag = yrs 2 − 16 $CF = (YPF_n)(PVF_L)$ $\quad = (YPF_{15})(PVF_1)$	$\begin{aligned} &\ 6.811 \\ \times\ &\ 0.8929 \\ =\ &\ 6.0815 \end{aligned}$	$+19\,461$
Balancing adjustment Asset life < project life hence WDV = 0 but RV = 0 hence BA = 0	—	—
Income £40K per annum Yrs 1–20	7.469	$+298\,760$
Corporation tax £40K pa @ 40% tax $= (40)(0.40)$ $= £16K$ 1 yr tax lag = yrs 2–21 $= (YPF_{20})(PVF_1)$	$\begin{aligned} &\ 7.469 \\ \times\ &\ 0.8929 \\ =\ &\ 6.6691 \end{aligned}$	$-106\,706$
	NPV =	$+37\,025$

Here the balancing adjustment is nil, because the project has been written-down to zero before the end of its actual life, and it has no residual value. The result shows a positive NPV at 12 per cent discount rate, indicating a profitability over 20 years of at least 12 per cent per annum tax paid.

Had the project life been 10 years instead of 20, the balancing adjustment would have been as follows:

Cash flow	Discount factor	DCF £
Balancing adjustment Asset life 15 yrs Project life 10 yrs WDV = E − [(IA × E) + n(WDA × E]) = 200 − [(0·40 × 200) + 10(0·04 × 200)] = 200 − (80 + 80) = £40K WDV BA = WDV − RV = 40 − 0 = £40K @ 40% tax = £16K = bal allowance yr 10 　　lagged to yr 11	0·2875	+4 600

Here the written-down value at the end of the project life has not yet reached zero, and is still worth £40K. Since the residual value is nil, the £40K is allowed against corporation tax as a balancing allowance, the actual cash flow being a product of the balancing allowance of £40K and the tax rate of 40 per cent, giving a positive cash flow of £4·6K.

Yield rate with tax and allowances
In this last NPV example it was found that the project had a positive NPV when discounted at 12 per cent, indicating a profitability of at least this rate. To find the actual rate of profitability we calculate the DCF yield rate by means of trial discounting in the usual way.

It will not be necessary to calculate a target rate by means of the search reduction formula in this case, because we already know from the NPV analysis that the rate is something in excess of 12 per cent. We can therefore take 12 per cent as the lower rate and try an increase of (say) 5 per cent for our next rate, making this 17 per cent.

In order to calculate the IRR we now repeat the PV analysis, re-arranging the items into the order (i) cash outflow items, and (ii) cash inflow items, so that we may find the ratios as before described, prior to interpolation of the IRR at unity.

We proceed as follows:

EXAMPLE 17

Cash flow	12% factor	PV £	17% factor	PV £
Outflow Investment Yr 0	1	200 000	1	200 000
Tax £40K pa @ 40% tax = £16K lagged yrs 2–21	7·469 × 0·8929		5·628 × 0·9547	
	6·6691	106 706	4·8103	76 965
Cash outflow		306 706		276 965
Inflow Initial allowance 40% of £200K @ 40% tax = £32K yr 2	0·7972	25 510	0·7305	23 376
WD allowance 4% of £200K @ 40% tax = £3·2K lagged yrs 2–16	6·811 × 0·8929		5·324 × 0·8547	
	6·0815	19 461	4·5504	14 561
Balancing adjustment	—	—	—	—
Income £40K pa Yrs 1–20	7·469	298 760	5·628	225 120
Cash inflow		343 731		263 057

Cash flow	12% factor	PV £	17% factor	PV £
Ratios		306 706		276 965
		343 731		263 057
		= 0·892		= 1·053

Interpolation

$$\text{IRR} = L\% + \left[\frac{1·0 - LR}{HR - LR}\right](H\% - L\%)$$

$$= 12\% + \frac{1·0 - 0·892}{1·053 - 0·892} \times 5$$

$$= 12\% + 3·35$$

$$= 15·35\% \text{ yield rate}$$

Thus the actual rate of profitability is approximately $15\frac{1}{4}$ per cent, and it would now be interesting to compare this with the calculated rate if we ignore taxation altogether. In which case we should have an investment of £200K with a straightforward £40K per annum income; so that the cash flow profile would be a regular annuity, and we can use the equation:

$$\text{YPF} = \frac{\text{capital}}{\text{annuity}}$$

Substituting, we obtain:

$$\text{YPF} = \frac{200}{40} = 5·000$$

Now find 5·000 in the YP table against 20 years.
From tables:

yrs	18%	19%	20%	21%
20	5·353	5·101	4·870	4·657

Reading across at year 20 we find that 5·000 falls at just over 19 per cent, instead of the $15\frac{1}{4}$ per cent actually achieved.

If this project was not subject to any capital allowances, the difference between pre-tax and after-tax profitability would be even greater, the after-tax yield rate being calculated by trial discounting as before, but ignoring the tax allowances. The selection of trial rates in this case is still a fairly obvious choice, since we know the target rate must be lower than $15\frac{1}{4}$ per cent. We do not know how much lower however, so it might be quicker in the long run therefore to use our search reduction formula in this instance, as follows:

$$YPF_t = \frac{E \times L}{\sum CF}$$

$$= \frac{200 \times 20}{20(40 - 40\%)} = \frac{4000}{480}$$

$$= 8\cdot333$$

Now find 8·333 in the YP table against 20 years.
From tables:

yrs	9%	10%	11%
20	9·129	8·514	7·963

Reading across at year 20 we find that 8·333 is between 10 per cent and 11 per cent. The actual rate is likely to be a little higher than this due to the effect of tax lag, so that 10 per cent and 12 per cent should straddle the target.

Cash flow	10% factor	PV £	12% factor	PV £
Outflow				
Investment				
Yr 0	1	200 000	1	200 000
Tax				
£16K yrs 2–21	8·514		7·469	
	× 0·9091		× 0·8929	
	7·7401	123 842	6·6691	106 706
Cash outflow		323 842		306 706
Inflow				
Income £40K pa				
Yrs 1–20	8·514	340 560	7·469	298 760
Ratios		323 842		306 706
		340 560		298 760
		= 0·951		= 1·027

Interpolation

$$\text{IRR} = 10\% + \frac{1 \cdot 0 - 0 \cdot 951}{1 \cdot 027 - 0 \cdot 951} \times 2$$
$$= 10\% + 1 \cdot 29$$
$$= 11 \cdot 29\% \text{ yield rate}$$

As calculated above, the rate of profitability on, say, an office block, not attracting capital allowances, would therefore be 11¼ per cent, as against 15¼ per cent if the same project were an industrial building attracting capital allowances. When ignoring tax we obtained the misleadingly high figure of 19 per cent—which illustrates the desirability of taking taxation into account when conducting yield rate feasibility studies which are intended to be helpful rather than misleading. Admittedly, where tax affects all projects equally, the ranking order is not changed if taxation is ignored. However, unless the tax situation is considered very carefully in each case that it applies, and a full DCF analysis with taxation is then carried out where appropriate, it may well be that projects with positive NPVs are in fact lossmakers which have merely the appearance of viable projects with profitability above the cut-off rate.

Pre-project finance with tax

One item for consideration in a DCF appraisal which aims to be as accurate as the available data will allow is the question of pre-project finance. This was dealt with in principle in Chapter 4, but it must now be re-examined in order to see its effect upon yield rate analysis. It will be recalled that pre-project finance entails the compounding of cash flows prior to year 0, which affects both land acquisition and building contract cash flows.

When conducting a PV analysis, these cash flows are usually compounded at the discount rate, which may or may not be the actual borrowing rate. In yield rate calculation the logical rate to use is the internal rate of return, ie, the trial discount rates. It may be thought that one should always use the actual borrowing rate, but this is not necessarily so appropriate as it may appear, because:

(i) if the borrowing rate in PV analysis differs from the discount rate, the question arises regarding interest payments on the loan *after* year 0,

(ii) the internal rate of return is so-called because it theoretically excludes consideration of extraneous sources and uses of finance, and

(iii) compounding of cash flows prior to year 0 is used conventionally simply as a device to avoid shifting the base year.

When so used, the discount (or trial discount) rate is obviously the correct one, and the consequences of using a different rate for pre-project finance really brings in the whole question of *dual rate* analysis, which will be discussed in the next chapter.

Meanwhile, it should be noted that, for tax purposes, the 'cost of building' includes quantity surveyor's and design fees, but not loan interest repayments in any calculation of the initial and writing-down allowances (though loan interest repayments may be allowable as a tax-free expense, where they arise). Hence the net figure is taken when calculating capital allowances, not the compounded cash flow at year 0.

The following is a simple illustration of trial discounting which involves compounding of pre-project cash flows.

EXAMPLE 18

Problem

Calculate the yield rate over 15 years of a small office block development allowing for corporation tax at the rate of 40 per cent, no investment incentives being allowable. Assume the following data:

Cost of site including fees £20K, acquired 3 years prior to contract completion
Building contract £75K including fees, with a two-year contract period
Income from rents £30K per annum
Tax lag 2 years
K = 1000.

Solution

Calculation of the target rate

	£K
Sum of cash flows:	
Income 15 × £30K	450
less tax @ 40%	180
	270
Investment:	
Site	20
Building	75
	95

Life: 15 years + (say) 2 = 17 yrs

$$YPF_t = \frac{E \times L}{\Sigma CF}$$

$$= \frac{95 \times 17}{270} = 5.9815$$

From the YP table we find that, reading across at year 17 the factor 6·047 gives 15 per cent target rate. This should be slightly exceeded because of the two-year tax lag.

Note that the 'life' taken in the above target calculation was 17 years; an approximation of the total life assessed as from a point prior to year 0 when the bulk of the initial investment is paid. Let us try 14 per cent and 16 per cent for discounting, using a mid-point for the building contract (year minus 1) and compounding minus years from the 'Amount of Pound' (compound interest) tables, as follows.

Cash flow		14% factor	*PV* £	16% factor	*PV* £
Outflow					
Site £20K					
Yr −3		1·482	29 640	1·561	31 220
Building £75K					
Yr −1		1·140	85 500	1·160	87 000
Tax					
£30K pa @ 40% tax					
= £12K yrs 3–17		6·142		5·575	
	×	0·7695		× 0·7432	
		4·7263	56 716	4·1433	49 720
Cash outflow			171 856		167 940
Inflow					
Income £30K pa		6·142	184 260	5·575	167 250
Ratios			171 856		167 940
			184 260		167 250
		=	0·933	=	1·004

As can be seen from the results, 16 per cent discounts to 1·004, which is close enough to unity to regard it as the internal rate of return (interpolation gives 15·89 per cent).

Tax-free negative cash flows
As previously indicated, certain expenses incurred in the pursuit of trade by companies coming under the charge of corporation tax are allowable against taxation, and where a development company incurs maintenance charges and running costs, these may be allowable items, as might other expenses such as agent's commission etc.

For example, let us suppose in the above case that the developer and not the tenant was responsible for certain annual running costs, amounting to an estimated figure of £2000 per annum. If we were to ignore tax relief, this would require an entry on the DCF analysis as follows:

Cash flow	14% factor	PV £	16% factor	PV £
Running costs: £2K pa yrs 1–15	6·142	12 284	5·575	11 150

In taking tax relief into consideration we shall need to adjust the cash flow by means of the formula referred to at the beginning of this chapter, as follows:

Cash flow	14% factor	PV £	16% factor	PV £
Running costs: £2K pa net of tax @ 40%. ACF $= M[100\% - (T\% \times PVF_L)]$ $= 2[100\% - (40\% \times PVF_2)]$ @ 14%: $= 2[100\% - (40\% \times 0\cdot7695)]$ $= 2(100\% - 30\cdot78\%)$ $= 2(0\cdot6922) = £1\cdot384K$	6·142	8 501		
@ 16%: $= 2[100\% - (40\% \times 0\cdot7432)]$ $= 2(100\% - 29\cdot728\%)$ $= 2(0\cdot7027) = £1\cdot405K$			5·575	7 833

This reduces the discounted cash flows to an amount reflecting the tax relief, and at the same time takes account of the fact that the tax relief itself (though not the running costs) is lagged by, in this case, two years.

Tax relief on periodic costs
Where periodic maintenance costs arise, the present value of such costs has been given as:

$$\sum(PVF \times C_p)$$

where C_p is any periodic cost.

Where a periodic cost is a recurring cost of uniform magnitude however, as with (say) redecorating every 5 years at an estimated cost of £5K, C_p becomes a constant, and the equation can be written:

$$PV = (\sum PVF)(C_p)$$

8

allowing the short cut of summating the PV factors and multiplying the result by the periodic cost, instead of multiplying out separately.

When adjusting for tax, we first modify the cash flow c_p by means of the tax adjustment formula, and then a cast can be formed of the PV factors, as in the following example, illustrating the entry in respect of a five-year running cost over a thirty-year period (including the thirtieth year), with a 40 per cent tax, lagged two years.

Cash flow		10% factor	DCF £
Maintenance: £5K every 5 yrs net of tax @ 40% ACF = 5[100 − (40% × PVF_2)] = 5[100% − (40% × 0·8264)] = 5(100% − 33·056%) = 5(0·6694) = £3·347K			
PV = (PVF) (C_p)	PVF yr 5	0·6209	
	10	0·3855	
	15	0·2394	
	20	0·1486	
	25	0·0923	
	30	0·0573	
£3·347K	×	1·5440	5168

Agent's commission

Tax relief may also be obtainable on the agent's commission when this is incurred as a necessary expense of trade by a development company subject to corporation tax. Where this is in respect of letting for example, the entry might be as follows.

Cash flow		10% factor	PV £
Agent's commission: 10% of 1 yrs rent = 10% of £30K net of tax = £3K net of tax = 3[100% − (40% × 0·8264)] = 3(0·6694) = £2·008K yr 0		1	2008

Balancing adjustments and capital gains

As we have seen, in projects attracting a depreciation allowance the residual value requires estimating in order to calculate the probable balancing allowance. But this residual value will of course also be a positive cash flow in its own right (see Figure 7 (*a*), Chapter 7), and its tax liability will need to be considered.

The sale of a fixed asset is not considered to be taxable income for the purpose of corporation tax and will therefore not attract a tax charge as such. The question of *capital gains tax* arises however, if the disposal figure of the asset exceeds its original cost. Capital gains tax is now amalgamated with corporation tax, which is payable on capital gains at the corporation tax rate. In the case of a building sold for a figure higher than the cost of building, corporation tax will be payable on the difference.

As previously indicated, balancing charges are limited to the amount of previous allowances: that is, the cost of building minus the WDV. Now we have seen that:

$$BA = WDV - RV$$

where BA is an allowance where positive, and a charge where negative. This is the same as saying:

$$\text{balancing charge} = RV - WDV$$

where the sign is changed on both sides. The limitation of the balancing charge to the amount of the allowances is equivalent to:

$$\text{limit} = E - WDV$$

where E is the investment (cost of building) and WDV the written-down value of the asset. Thus we could say:

$$BC = RV - WDV \text{ provided } BC \not> E - WDV$$

When the balancing charge is greater than $E - WDV$, the difference must be a capital gain, since the RV is then greater than E. The simple example shown below will clarify the relationship between balancing charge and capital gain.

EXAMPLE 19

Problem

An industrial building cost £100K and is sold for £150K. When sold, its written-down value for the purpose of capital allowances is £30K. Calculate the balancing charge and the amount of capital gain.

$K = 1000$.

Solution

	£K	£K
Cost of building	100	
Residual value		150
Written-down value	32	32
	68	118
balancing charge		68
capital gain		50

If the written-down value had been zero, the previous allowances would have equalled the cost of building, and the balancing charge would then be limited to this amount. The capital gain would remain the same however, as follows:

Capital gain where WDV = 0:

	£K	£K
Cost of building	100	
Residual value		150
Written-down value	0	0
	100	150
balancing charge		100
capital gain		50

Capital gains made by companies are chargeable to corporation tax, as are balancing charges. So it would appear that, from the above examples, the negative cash flow amounts to £150K in any case, made up partly from balancing charges and partly from tax on capital gains, both at the rate of corporation tax. So why separate the two charges?

Apart from the fact that capital gains, but not balancing adjustments, may apply to the land as well as the building, the reason for considering capital gains cash flows separately from balancing charges is that they may well be treated by the Inland Revenue in slightly different ways in individual cases, owing to financial and other circumstances of the company at the time. In particular, certain 'roll-over' provisions may enable the company to defer tax payment on capital gains though not on balancing charges for example. But to delve more deeply than this into the ramifications of company taxation is outside the scope of this book, and the reader is referred to the various taxation publications issued from time to time by the Board of Inland

Revenue for further information. Meanwhile, the following brief observations will suffice for present purposes.

Capital allowances may be 'actual' or 'notional', and may be affected by change of ownership (only actual allowances count when calculating limitations). This and many other factors make corporation tax cash flows difficult to predict with any real accuracy, especially towards the end of a project's life. Hence there is a case for keeping calculations as simple as possible, and avoiding the complexities which occur when trying to achieve an appearance of complete accuracy in what after all is only an estimated future cash flow profile. This does not mean that we should not attempt to make our data and calculations as accurate as circumstances allow; merely that a sense of proportion should be observed, especially in the light of the fact that cash flows in the distant future (such as residual values and balancing adjustments) have less effect on present values than do those in the near future, because of the differential consequences of the discounting mechanism. The higher the discount rate, the lesser the importance to be attached to cash flows in the distant future, since they lose greater value in the process of discounting procedures.

Bearing in mind the above factors, the entry on the DCF analysis for residual values in respect of the last example (assuming the land cost £40K and is sold at an apportioned value of £80K) might be as follows.

Cash flow				10% factor	DCF £
Residual value:					
	£K	£K			
Building		150			
Land		80			
		230	yr 7	0·5132	+118 036
Building cost	100				
Land cost	40	140			
Capital gain		90			
£90K @ 40% tax lagged 1 yr = (90) (0·40) = £36K			yr 8	0·4665	−16 794

In the example the balancing charge of £70K is assumed to be dealt with by means of a separate entry in the usual way. It is also assumed that the capital allowances were such as to show the written-down value of £32K in year 7 when the property was sold. But as can be seen, the WDV does not affect the capital gains cash flows, only the balancing adjustment.

Chapter 9
Ancillary factors

In the last three chapters an attempt was made to explain the mechanism of yield rate analysis in relation to feasibility studies of development projects, and to show how corporation tax and allowances may be taken into consideration when carrying out discounted cash flow calculations. In this present chapter some additional factors will be discussed which may need to be taken into account when preparing or interpreting the results of such appraisals.

The effect of inflation

The examples previously given in this book have all ignored the possible effects of future inflation of the economy; but the steadily falling value of money appears to be a fact of economic life, and no doubt the reader who has progressed so far will have asked himself how inflation might affect the validity of such exercises.

When ranking projects by comparison of their net present values, it can be argued that inflation will have an equal effect on the projects being ranked, and will therefore have no effect on the ranking order. Again, since inflation appears to affect both the negative and the positive cash flows to an equal extent, it might be argued that its effect will cancel out, and not change the numerical values of the results. Another line of argument is that, since it is the present-day values which are being compared, future inflation of the economy is irrelevant, as it does not affect the present-day situation.

For the above reasons inflation effect is frequently ignored in DCF calculations, another reason being the inherent difficulty of predicting what the relevant inflation rate is likely to be in, say, ten years time. Or for that matter, in a year's time!

However, there are circumstances where it might be desirable to take account of inflation in feasibility appraisals, in particular where inflation is thought likely to have a differential effect. For example, in a case where no rent review provisions apply, the income would remain fixed, but costs would rise with inflation. Or again, inflation might have a greater effect on some cash flows than on others, a typical instance being in the case of maintenance costs. Since maintenance work tends to be labour-intensive, it tends to inflate ahead of new building work and other costs, and in an appraisal where this factor is thought to be significant, an inflation rate is sometimes allowed for on maintenance costs only, as well as on other items of probable expenditure thought to be in a similar category.

Differential inflation
In such cases allowance may be made for inflation by differential adjustment of the discount rates. In order to adjust the discount rate for inflation in respect of a particular cash flow in NPV analysis, we need to distinguish between positive and negative cash flows. To adjust a negative cash flow (eg, a maintenance cost), the following formula is appropriate:

$$AR_n = \left(\frac{100 + m}{100 + R} - 1 \right) \times 100$$

where AR_n = adjusted rate (negative cash flow)
$\quad$ m $\quad$ = money rate (discount rate)
$\quad$ R $\quad$ = inflation rate
The above formula *reduces* the discount rate, thus increasing the present value of the (negative) cash flow and reducing the NPV.

Should we wish to allow for inflation of a positive cash flow, the formula is changed to:

$$AR_p = \frac{(100 + m)(100 + R)}{100} - 100$$

where AR_p = adjusted rate (positive cash flow)
This last formula *increases* the discount rate, thus reducing the present value of the (positive) cash flow and increasing the NPV.

Adjusting the yield rate
It is possible to allow for the effect of inflation on the internal rate of return, where earnings subsequent to year 0 have not been adjusted to real purchasing-power terms. This is done by adjusting the yield rate to allow for the reduction of NPV due to inflation effect, by means of the following formula:

$$AY = \left(\frac{100 + Y}{100 + R} - 1 \right) \times 100$$

where AY = adjusted yield
$\quad$ Y $\quad$ = yield rate
$\quad$ R $\quad$ = inflation rate
This assumes an investment in year 0 and no subsequent net negative cash flows, and is the same formula as that used to adjust negative cash flows when discounting in order to reduce their discount rate and increase their present values.

Interest rate inflation
Increases in the general rate of inflation tend to push up the cost of capital by increasing loan interest rates and investment rates generally. With NPV

analysis it may be possible to allow for this by increasing the discount rate, and in yield rate analysis by increasing the reinvestment rate. The PROSPER computer program, mentioned in the next chapter, allows for time-variable discount rates to be specified, enabling the computer to take into account periodic changes in the discount rate due, for example, to inflation effect. Thus one can extrapolate past changes in investment rates into the future and obtain results accordingly. Constant rates are generally used when discounting manually, owing to the difficulty of variable-rate discounting by hand. This problem is overcome by computer working; but not, unfortunately, the problem of predicting accurately what changes, if any, will actually occur in the rate of inflation in future years.

Interest on loan capital

The internal rate of return is the calculated annual rate of return on the capital outstanding in a project. Thus it does not basically take account of the loan interest rate, if any, on the capital employed. However, any interest on the loan may be deducted from the calculated IRR, giving an IRR net of loan interest. This assumes that loan capital is repayable at will, the interest being on the reducing balance, as in the case of a joint stock bank overdraft. Interest on capital loans may be allowable against corporation tax; but if it is not, the loan interest rate used will need to be an after-tax rate.

Multiple solutions

Under certain conditions it is possible that there may be more than one yield rate which makes the PV of future cash flows equal the investment. This would seem to undermine the concept of IRR altogether; but provided the possible conditions which can bring this state of affairs about are known and recognised, the true rate of return can be found in such cases, and no harm done. The conditions under which such multiple solutions may arise do not occur often in practice, but it is as well to be on guard against the eventuality.

Multiple solutions may come into play when, from any point in the project onwards, the sum of the cash flows is negative, or the cumulative total of present values changes its sign back to negative during the life of the project. This is only likely to occur when there is a heavy negative outflow at some point in the life of the project. Where such a cash flow profile exists, the cash flows should be inspected, and the point from which the cumulative total changes its sign determined. From this point onwards the cash flows are then discounted at the earning rate back to a point where they are absorbed by the previous positive cash flows, and the DCF analysis is then carried out in the normal manner using the revised cash flow profile.

The following cash flow pattern has not only multiple exact solutions, but an *infinite number* of almost exact solutions, in the lower ranges of percentages.

yrs	0	1	2	3
£K	−100	+360	−410	+150

It will be observed that the PV of the cash flows changes from negative to positive and *back to negative* again, this being a criterion of multiple yield possibility. Also in this case the NPV of the cash flows discounted at zero equals nought, meaning that one yield solution rate must be zero.

Misleading yield rates

Consider the following cash flow pattern:

yr	0	1	2	3	4	5	6	7
£K	−400	+300	+200	+200	+159	+100	+100	−900

This cash flow has a yield rate of 30 per cent, but when discounted at a *lower* rate shows a *positive* NPV. This is because it has a negative NPV when discounted at zero per cent. What is happening here is that the large outflow in year 7 is so reduced by discounting as to turn the project into a profitable one if discounted at a high enough rate. At a lower rate, the project is a loss-maker. Thus where a project has a negative NPV when discounted at zero per cent, the yield solution rate may be theoretically correct and also unique, but hardly a valid ranking criterion when comparing the project with other projects which have different cash flow patterns giving a positive NPV at zero per cent.

Thus we may conclude that a yield rate is suspect as a valid criterion if (*a*) the cumulative total of present values changes to positive and back again to negative, or (*b*) the cash flows have a negative NPV when discounted at zero per cent. These conditions are both brought about by net negative cash flows occurring during, or at the end of, the life of the project.

Dual rate analysis

In the last two cash flow profiles we saw, respectively, (*a*) a change of sign in the cumulative NPV, and (*b*) a heavy negative cash flow at the end of the project. Either circumstance may make the yield rate misleading unless surplus cash flows are discounted at the earning rate, as previously described. This is because, when heavy negative cash flows occur at or towards the end of the project, the project is building up a sinking-fund to offset these during the period when the NPV is positive. This sinking-fund is being discounted at the yield rate however, instead of at a more realistic earning rate, thus invalidating results.

If therefore a specific rate of interest is stipulated for reinvestment of surplus funds, and surplus cash flows discounted at this reinvestment rate, the yield rate will not only be unique, but meaningful and realistic at the same time. This is known as dual rate analysis.

It is emphasised however that ordinary single-rate yield analysis may be regarded as satisfactory in the majority of cases. Dual rate analysis only becomes necessary when inspection of the cash flows reveals the possibility of multiple solutions or an otherwise misleading yield rate. Nevertheless, it has been claimed that dual rate analysis is a more realistic measure of profitability in any case than single rate yield. It is best carried out on the computer, as described in the next chapter.

Dual rate tables

Parry's Valuation Tables contain both single rate and dual rate years purchase tables, and it may be thought that in discounting cash flows the use of dual rate tables might, in certain cases at least, be more realistic than the use of single rate tables.

Now the two rates involved in dual rate years purchase are (i) the interest rate on the loan, and (ii) the interest on sinking-fund instalments. When an actual sinking-fund is set aside to redeem the loan, the rate is likely to be lower than the loan interest rate because gilt-edged security will be required. Hence the concept of differential rates.

However, as we saw in Chapter 2 in connection with the PV method, in DCF analysis we use the YP table merely as a device for calculating the present value of one pound per annum at the discount rate, and the concept of a separate sinking-fund does not therefore arise. Thus in the context of discounted cash flow, the use of dual rate YP tables is not an appropriate method when calculating present values.

Valuation tables with tax allowance

The valuation tables contain PV, YP and ASF tables with allowance for tax. The years purchase tables with tax allowance are confined to dual rate tables only, which allow for the effect of income tax on that part of the income used to provide the annual sinking-fund instalment. But dual rate YP tables have been seen above to be inappropriate to PV discounting, so need detain us no further.

The PV and ASF tables with tax allowance give results which make allowance for the effect of tax on interest accumulations, and where this applies, the use of these tables in PV discounting would appear to be appropriate. It may be more convenient however to allow for the tax on interest accumulations by adjusting the rate of interest by means of the formula:

$$NR = GR \left(\frac{100 - T\%}{100} \right)$$

where NR = net rate
      GR = gross rate
      T% = tax rate

This has the same effect as using the tax tables where only PV (or ASF) tables are used in an appraisal, but it also adjusts annuity cash flows where these occur.

Chapter 10
Computer analysis

Discounted cash flow calculations, carried out with suitable discount tables, and aided by a little practice and the help of a search-reduction formula, will generally incur only a small burden of arithmetical computation. It will usually be found accurate enough to round seven-figure present value factors to four, or even three decimal places, and log tables can be used for the occasional awkward long division, or a slide rule when considerations of accuracy permit. Better still, an electronic desk or pocket calculator (preferably with automatic floating-point) will be found to greatly increase speed and accuracy of working, and relieve the strain of manual working in the case of complex analyses involving trial runs and careful checking of arithmetic. This is especially true where discrepancies are suspected or multiple solutions need to be avoided.

In some cases it will be found worthwhile to run an analysis on the computer, and this will not only enable accurate results to be obtained very quickly, but will also allow calculations to be performed which may be considered outside the scope of manual working altogether, even with tables and calculating machines. For example, it may be a relatively simple matter to calculate the yield rate by trial discounting (including taxation) of a project with a fifty-year life by manual methods. But to find the yield rate for each year would be another matter. And if we could do this, we could see at a glance the profitability profile over the whole life of the project, when it starts to make a profit, how much if terminated earlier than fifty years, etc. This would be a formidable task to do manually by trial discounting, but the computer can do it in a matter of minutes.

The computer can also carry out other operations, such as calculating payback periods, performing dual rate and variable rate analysis, giving probability appreciations, supplying alternative solutions by varying the parameters, etc. Many such operations are usually not feasible by manual working in the time available, but the computer can carry them out with ease, as a by-product of automatic yield rate calculation.

This chapter will attempt to describe some computer systems available for use in this field, starting with a simple cash flow analysis program, proceeding to a more sophisticated system incorporating taxation facilities, and concluding with a brief description of systems offering a more complex range of applications.

111

CASH FLOW ANALYSIS PROGRAM

This program is written in FORTRAN IV for an IBM 1130 installation with card input. It has been written mainly for teaching purposes and its simplicity makes its description a suitable introduction to the subject for those readers who may be unfamiliar with computer working.

The Cash Flow Analysis program (CFA) can do three things: calculate either (*a*) the net present value; (*b*) the yield rate (internal rate of return); or (*c*) the yield rate after repayment of loan interest.

If the NPV is required, a discount rate must be supplied. Otherwise CFA will calculate the yield rate, on an ordinary single-rate basis, net of loan interest if required.*

CFA input

The computer requires to know (i) the cash flows with their year numbers, (ii) the discount rate (if NPV required), and (iii) the loan interest rate (if net yield required). Input is by means of standard eighty-column punched cards, arranged into 'decks' as follows:

    (1) control cards
    (2) program cards
    (3) header card
    (4) data cards
    (5) last card

The control, program, and header cards set up the computer to receive the data cards. The data cards contain the cash flows, including the investment, year numbers, and discount and loan interest rates (if required). The data must be punched in correct format on the cards, as follows.

Card 1. Job title: columns 1–60. Discount rate: columns 65–70. Loan interest rate: columns 75–80. Job title optional length up to 60 digits. Rate columns may be left blank.

Card 2. Cash flow: columns 1–10. Year number: right justified in columns 16–18 (must be an integer number). Negative cash flows (investment) to be preceded by a minus sign.

Cards 3–52. As card 2 above. Optional for any number of years up to 50.

The cash flow figures and the discount and loan interest rates must contain a decimal point: that is, in columns 1–8, 65–68 and 75–78 respectively. The year numbers must not contain a decimal point. The cash flow cards (2–52)

*CFA is the copyright of David Hembury, Department of Building & Civil Engineering. Southampton College of Technology, to whom any enquiries regarding the program should be addressed.

represent one card for each year up to 50 years (including year 0), but less than 50 cards are acceptable, eg, a five year life requires only six cards (including the one for year 0).

At the end of the data cards, a separate 'last card' is placed. This is in the form of a blank card, which tells the computer that the data is complete and processing is to begin.

From the above it will be evident that CFA handles a project life of up to 50 years, but this can be increased by amending the program.

The compounding of any pre-project cash flows can be dealt with by prior manipulation of the data, but if compounding is to be at the yield rate, the first negative cash flow is punched on the first cash flow card, thus setting back the year scale. Any cash flow card will accept a minus sign, permitting input of negative cash flows at any point in the year scale, eg, a final tax payment on capital gains. Prior manipulation of the data can also be used to deal with taxation adjustments, running costs, etc, the resultant net cash flows being punched on the cash flow cards.

CFA output

Output from the line-printer comprises a table giving the year number, the cash flow, the present value factor, and the NPV in respect of each year. Also the cumulative net present values, for inspection of possible sign changes during the life of the project. In the case of a yield calculation, the yield rate is printed out, either gross or net, depending on whether a loan interest rate has been stipulated. With NPV calculation, the stipulated discount rate is printed instead. An example of the yield printout is illustrated in Figure 8.

The yield rate calculated by CFA as the program stands is restricted to a range of −5 per cent to +25 per cent, but this range can be increased by program modification.

Conclusions

CFA is a basic teaching program offering restricted facilities, but is useful when accurate solution of the DCF yield is required, especially on a project with a relatively long life and an irregular cash flow profile, requiring extensive trial discounting.

ANALYSIS OF CAPITAL INVESTMENT

Program for Analysis of Capital Investment (PACIN) is an IBM commercial program for use, like CFA, on an IBM 1130 installation. The program itself is supplied by IBM and made available to IBM computer users.

The facilities offered by PACIN include a rate of return for each year of the project on a single or dual-rate basis, with certain automatic tax calculations if required, together with input of regular cash flow profiles on a single card, plus various additional options, including a probability estimate.

C A S H   F L O W   A N A L Y S I S

SAMPLE YIELD RATE PRINTOUT

YEAR	CASH FLOW	PRESENT VALUE FACTOR	DISCOUNTED CASH FLOW	CUMULATIVE PRESENT VALUE
0	-6421.52	1.000000	-6421.52	-6421.52
1	875.25	0.906453	793.37	-5628.14
2	923.00	0.821658	758.39	-4869.75
3	765.64	0.744795	570.24	-4299.50
4	966.33	0.675123	652.39	-3647.11
5	658.22	0.611968	402.80	-3244.30
6	885.60	0.554720	491.26	-2753.04
7	468.10	0.502829	235.37	-2517.67
8	922.06	0.455791	420.23	-2097.43
9	776.55	0.413153	320.83	-1776.59
10	556.00	0.374504	208.22	-1568.37
11	687.53	0.339471	233.39	-1334.97
12	997.00	0.307715	306.79	-1028.18
13	586.97	0.278929	163.72	-864.46
14	789.88	0.252837	199.71	-664.75
15	932.12	0.229185	213.62	-451.12
16	468.95	0.207745	97.42	-353.69
17	967.88	0.188311	182.26	-171.43
18	1023.85	0.170696	174.76	3.33
19	885.00	0.154728	136.93	140.26
20	-1000.00	0.140253	-140.25	0.01

THE YIELD RATE = 10.32

Figure 8

PACIN input

The data required by the computer is divided into two kinds, (*a*) *basic data*, input on the first data card, and (*b*) *secondary data*, some of which is optional, on subsequent cards.

The basic data comprises:

(1) *Investment.* Total capital required in year 0. Maximum value 99999999.

(2) *Project life.* Maximum of 50 years.

(3) *Tax rate.* Maximum value 99 per cent. A zero tax rate may be used when this facility is not required.

(4) *Project description.* An optional job title of up to 35 digits, to be included in the printout.

The basic data is followed by a 'mode' card, giving instructions to the computer as to the mode of operations to be carried out in respect of the secondary data which is to follow. This secondary data is input in strict format and sequence, but is dealt with here in the order thought to be most appropriate in clarifying the general workings of the system and giving the clearest picture of its facilities.

Rate of return

The secondary data in respect of the rate of return comprises the optional input of a reinvestment rate, which has the effect of creating a dual-rate analysis. If the parameter on the 'mode' card is set to 1, ordinary single-rate yield is calculated by the computer, and no secondary data is required for the rate of return. By setting the mode parameter to 2 however, the yield rate is calculated by annual discounting with reinvestment of the net cash flow at the rate input as secondary data.

The reinvestment rate may be input to two decimal places, up to a maximum of 99·99 per cent.

Cash flow values

The cash flows may be input in a number of different ways, depending on the general cash flow profile. Thus it is not necessary to prepare one card for each year unless the profile is irregular, and special provision is made for cash flow profiles following, for example, a straight-line decline, where income is estimated to decrease as the asset depreciates, or for other reasons. In all, five different options are given, and the mode parameter is set according to which one has been selected, as follows.

(1) *Uniform earnings.* Where income is in the form of an annuity (eg, from rents), the income figure per annum is punched on one card, and the computer assumes that this income continues during the life of the project. The maximum value is an eight-figure number for the annual amount.

(2) *Straight-line decline.* Again, a single card is prepared, but this time it must contain (i) the initial value of the income, (ii) the minimum value to which it is estimated the income will fall with the passage of time, and (iii) the time in years over which it falls (maximum time being the project life). The computer will then 'write down' the income on a straight-line basis until it reaches its minimum. All remaining values are then set equal to the final value.

(3) *Rapid early decline.* With certain types of income (eg, sales figures) an early fall-off might be thought probable, followed by a continual decline. In this case the computer performs a 'sum of years digits' calculation, similar to the one outlined in Chapter 7 for depreciation, resulting in a high-early straight-line cash flow, down to a stipulated minimum value.

(4) *Rapid later decline.* The opposite of (3) above, carried out by the computer using a 'reversed sum of years digits' technique.

(5) *Irregular cash flows.* With the parameter set to this option, it becomes necessary to punch one card for each year, as with CFA, each giving the required cash flow and year number. There must be one card for each year of the project life, and this particular option will be the one normally used for development project appraisals where any cash flow irregularity is introduced owing to periodic maintenance costs causing reduction of the otherwise constant income.

Taxation cash flows do not necessarily cause irregularity however, as these are provided for in the basic data. The same applies to residual values and tax depreciation allowances, provided for separately, as will be seen. Thus in some cases option (1) above may be used, even when tax and residual values are being taken into consideration, without any need for prior adjustment of the data. There are limitations to these facilities however (without program modification): for example, an initial allowance is not automatically provided for, making for cash flow irregularity where this is required to be taken into account.

Depreciation allowance
When the computer is required to take depreciation allowance against taxation into account, this may be achieved by input of a single card containing the necessary secondary data. There are four options for this, depending on the type of depreciation allowance involved.

(1) *Straight-line depreciation.* The secondary data required is simply (i) the percentage rate, and (ii) the number of years in which the investment is to be depreciated. The maximum number of years is the project life.

(2) *Declining balance.* Data required as for (1) above.

(3) *Sum of years digits.* As for (2) above.

(4) *Other methods of depreciation.* A card for each year of the project life may be used, with year numbers and depreciation values punched. The computer will then take these into account when calculating taxation cash flows.

It will be recalled that the tax rate is input with basic data, so that the computer has the means of calculating the depreciation allowance against taxation by any of the above methods. However, neither an initial allowance nor a balancing adjustment is specifically provided for, and tax lag is not automatically taken into account either. These factors might possibly be catered for in certain circumstances by using option (4) above (year numbers and values) or may be allowed for by prior manipulation of the cash flow data, or by a combination of both. For initial and writing-down allowances in the case of industrial buildings, the initial allowance can be dealt with by prior adjustment of the relevant cash flow, and the writing-down allowance by opting for the straight-line depreciation mode. Providing a balancing adjustment is not involved, this seems a very convenient method. Admittedly tax and allowance lag (where these apply) would not be accounted for by this method, but the resultant error would be on the right side, as it were, and the yield rate known to be slightly pessimistic on this account.

Residual value

There is an optional input of secondary data for residual (salvage or trade-in) value. The main idea behind this is to enable the computer to calculate what the residual value will eventually amount to. This amount is finally discounted at the yield rate and deducted from the initial investment by the computer. According to which parameter is set on the 'mode' card, the residual value is calculated by means of (*a*) straight-line decline, (*b*) exponential decline, or (*c*) book value. Alternatively, salvage values may be stipulated and year numbers given.

Loan repayment

It will be recalled that CFA includes a facility which computes a yield rate net of loan interest repayment. PACIN has a somewhat similar facility, but allows for repayment of loan interest plus repayment of the principal also. This means that mortgage repayments on property can be allowed for by the computer, and initial deposits are also taken care of since the program can accept less than a one hundred per cent loan. Options are as follows:

(1) *Principal and interest repayment.* This requires input of secondary data on one card comprising (i) percentage of invested capital which is borrowed; (ii) number of years over which the loan is to be repaid; and (iii) the rate of interest on the loan.

9

When the parameter is set to this mode, the computer calculates the yield net of mortgage repayments, even though the term may be less than the life of the project itself.

(2) *Repayment of principal only.* In this mode an annual repayment of the principal only is made, input of secondary data being as for (1) above.

(3) *Interest repayment.* Where repayment of the interest only is required, a card for each year is necessary, each containing the year number and the amount of interest to be repaid in that year.

Probability values

A facility is provided for inserting probability values in the secondary data to enable the computer to calculate the *expected* rate of return based on the *expected* net cash flow, which it displays by means of an additional line of output on the printout. This is achieved by punching a card containing a probability factor followed by an estimated average life for the project. There is a choice of factors allowed, ranging from pure obsolescence to no obsolescence, and from these the computer calculates a probability curve, and prints a table giving the probability of the life of the project being terminated in that particular year, as well as giving the expected rate of return for the project as a whole.

Net cash flow calculation

The mode parameters contain an option for calculating the cash flows net of loan interest (or capital and interest repayments) as stipulated by the loan repayment secondary data. This option causes the cash flow table to be printed not only less tax, but less tax and loan interest when required. Thus either cash flow less tax, or cash flow less tax and interest is displayed for each year, depending on the option selected.

PACIN output

Output is in the form of seven tables, plus an additional line of output giving the expected rate of return when the probability calculation has been utilised. The tables, as illustrated in a typical printout shown in Figure 9 are listed under the following headings:

(1) *Depr Tab.* This is the depreciation table, and shows the cash flow generated by the writing-down allowance against taxation, where this applies. The tax on earnings is reduced by this amount, which is added by the computer to the (net) cash flow column.

(2) *Salv Tab.* The salvage value (residual value) of the asset at the end of the current year is shown in this column, where applicable. This would be the value calculated by the computer on (say) an exponential decline basis from the optional secondary data.

```
TAL    INV LIFE  TAX RATE
000.        20.        40.    PROJECT 04036
S OF OPERATION
2 2 2 1 2
CENT  NO YEARS  FOR DEPRECIATION
  90.       12.
CENT  NO YEARS  MIN. VAL  FOR SALVAGE
  80.       15.     12500.
ORM EARNINGS
5000.
CENT  NO YEARS  INT RATE  FOR INTEREST
  20.        7.      725.
LES. AVE LIFE  FOR PROBABILITY
  75.       12.
```

DEPR TAB	SALV TAB	EARN TAB	INT TAB	CASH FLOW	PROB TAB	EARN RATE	YR
15000.	150167.	25000.	2900.	19260.	0.024	-15.29	1
15000.	140333.	25000.	2567.	19460.	0.029	-5.67	2
15000.	130500.	25000.	2211.	19674.	0.034	-2.09	3
15000.	120667.	25000.	1828.	19903.	0.039	-0.15	4
15000.	110833.	25000.	1418.	20149.	0.045	1.12	5
15000.	101000.	25000.	978.	20413.	0.050	2.07	6
15000.	91167.	25000.	506.	20696.	0.055	2.81	7
15000.	81333.	25000.	0.	21000.	0.059	3.45	8
15000.	71500.	25000.	0.	21000.	0.062	3.98	9
15000.	61667.	25000.	0.	21000.	0.065	4.45	10
15000.	51833.	25000.	0.	21000.	0.066	4.86	11
15000.	42000.	25000.	0.	21000.	0.066	5.24	12
0.	32167.	25000.	0.	15000.	0.065	5.36	13
0.	22333.	25000.	0.	15000.	0.062	5.48	14
0.	12500.	25000.	0.	15000.	0.059	5.61	15
0.	12500.	25000.	0.	15000.	0.055	6.04	16
0.	12500.	25000.	0.	15000.	0.050	6.41	17
0.	12500.	25000.	0.	15000.	0.045	6.73	18
0.	12500.	25000.	0.	15000.	0.039	7.00	19
0.	12500.	25000.	0.	15000.	0.034	7.25	20

```
CTED RATE OF RETURN      4.74
```

Figure 9

(3) *Earn Tab.* This is the earnings table, ie, a printout of income for each year as input by one of the options for punching of the cash flow profile. This is the column from which is computed the taxation, where a tax rate has been input in the basic data.

(4) *Int Tab.* This shows the interest paid on the loan during the current year, or interest plus principal, etc, according to the parameter set when selecting input data on loan repayment.

(5) *Cash Flow.* The net cash flow from which the internal rate of return is calculated.

(6) *Prob Tab.* Printout of factors showing the probability of ending the investment during the current year. Used only when probability factors have been input as secondary data.

(7) *Earn Rate.* The internal rate of return which would be realised on the investment if the project was terminated at the end of the current year. It may be either single rate or dual rate, according to whether reinvestment rate has been stipulated in the secondary data. It will be an after-tax rate of return if a tax rate has been stipulated in the basic data. It may be net of loan interest (or interest and capital repayment) if desired.

Conclusions
PACIN is a relatively sophisticated program offering a wide selection of optional facilities, including dual-rate analysis. It gives the yield rate for each year, and this enables one to see at a glance the profitability of the project as it progresses.

Taxation, straight-line or other forms of writing-down allowance, and uniform annual income do not require one card for each year, and this reduces data preparation time (and chances of data errors), especially significant in the case of long project lives.

The PACIN program was written by an IBM employee living in New York, and does not make special provision for such UK tax regulations as, for example, initial allowances, balancing allowances, tax and allowance lag, investment grants, etc. These can be accounted for however by prior manipulation of the data, or by program modification.

PROFIT RATING OF PROJECTS

Profit Rating Of Projects (PROP) is a commercial ICL package program written for the ICL 1900 computer. There are different versions of PROP available for different 1900 computer configurations, but these are basically similar to the one described below. Some versions of PROP allow for a maximum project life of 30 years, but a 60-year version (x4P4) is now available.

The facilities offered by PROP include single-card input of initial allowances, tax lag, investment grants, and even grant lag, where applicable. In addition, there is provision for two estimated changes in the rate of corporation tax during the life of the project, along with single or dual-rate yield, dual-rate NPV, printout of payback periods and average annual rates of return, and a probability option which takes into account alternative cash flow patterns and displays the probable yield by means of a histogram generated by an advanced mathematical technique known as Monte Carlo analysis.

The input requirements of PROP where full facilities are required are somewhat involved, and specially printed forms are available in pads from ICL to assist in the coding of the data prior to punching of cards. These are similar in principle to ordinary coding sheets, but contain various headings and a special arrangement of lines peculiar to PROP input requirements. With a little practice this method of input preparation on special forms can be mastered quite easily, and will be found to be quite a convenient means of data preparation.

PROP input
The structure of PROP input is arranged to provide three basic options in respect of any individual project:

(1) a single printout giving results for the cash flow in question

(2) a multiple printout giving results for a number of alternative cash flows and combination of possible taxation situations and other parameter changes

(3) a Monte Carlo probability analysis.

To facilitate this, input is entered on the same three coding forms whichever of the options is required. These pre-printed forms are illustrated in Figures 10, 11 and 12 and are designated *Forms 1, 2* and *3* respectively. They are designed to contain the following data for subsequent punching on cards (or paper tape) for input to the computer.

Form 1. This contains one *header card* and up to ten *tax class cards.* The header card contains basic data such as tax and grant lag, corporation tax rate (up to three different rates at different periods in one project available on option), and the basic time period (years, months, or other periods are available) for the appraisal.

Each tax class card contains data regarding investment incentives. Investment grant, initial allowance and annual (writing-down) allowance are provided for, with an optional change to a second annual allowance available. A 'method' digit gives the choice between straight-line or reducing-balance calculation of the annual allowance.

Up to ten tax class cards allow up to ten different combinations of investment incentives to be selected by the computer when a multiple printout is required.

Taxation and investme
incentive rates for

Project

Date

Prepared by

Checked by

Aspect of Project

Assumptions/Comments

No. Periods Per Annum	Tax Time Lag	Grant Time Lag	Corporation Tax Rate 1	No. of Periods	Corporation Tax Rate 2	No. of Periods	Corporation Tax Rate 3
1 2	3 4	5 6	7 10	11 12	13 16	17 18	19 22

Tax Class No.	Investment Cash Grant Rate	Initial Tax Allowance Rate	Annual Tax Allowance Rate 1	Method 1	Life Years 1	Annual Tax Allowance Rate 2	Method 2	Life Years 2
1 2	3 6	7 10	11 14	15	16 17	18 21	22	23 24

Figure 10 ICL PROP Form 1

Cash flow forecasts for

ct

Aspect of Project

ared by

ked by

Assumptions/Comments

Index No.	Last Form 2 Mk.	Probability of Forecast		Group Index No.	
2	3	4	6	7	8

Year		Period		Capital Amount										Operating Year			Tax Class No.			Revenue Amount							
		4	5	6	7								15	16		19	20	21	22								30

Figure 11 ICL PROP Form 2

Run selections for

Project   Aspect of Project
Date
Prepared by
Checked by   Assumptions/Comments

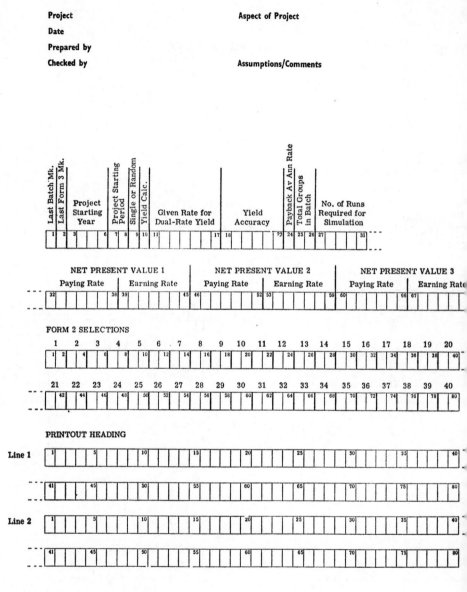

Figure 12 ICL PROP Form 3

PLANT EXPANSION - BRAND X.   ASSUMPTIONS - NO IN/DEFLATION OF COSTS/PRICES
GRANT 20%. ANNUAL ALLOW. 25%. REDUCING BALANCE FOR 5 YEARS. CORPORATION TAX 40%

YEAR	PERIOD	CAPITAL INVESTMENT	OTHER CAPITAL	INVESTMENT GRANT	INITIAL ALLOWANCE	ANNUAL ALLOWANCE	REVENUE INCOME	REVENUE COSTS	REVENUE PROFIT	TAX ON PROFIT	NET CASH FLOW
1966	3	-10000.0	0.0	0.0	0.0	0.0	0.0	-500.0	-500.0	0.0	-10500.0
	4	-2000.0	0.0	0.0	0.0	0.0	3000.0	-1000.0	2000.0	0.0	0.0
1967	1	0.0	0.0	0.0	0.0	0.0	2500.0	-1000.0	1500.0	0.0	1500.0
	2	0.0	0.0	0.0	0.0	0.0	2000.0	-1000.0	1000.0	0.0	1000.0
	3	0.0	0.0	0.0	0.0	800.0	3000.0	-1000.0	2000.0	-600.0	2200.0
	4	0.0	0.0	0.0	0.0	0.0	2500.0	-1000.0	1500.0	0.0	1500.0
1968	1	0.0	0.0	2000.0	0.0	0.0	2000.0	-1000.0	1000.0	0.0	3500.0
	2	0.0	0.0	0.0	0.0	600.0	3000.0	-1000.0	2000.0	+2400.0	1000.0
	3	0.0	0.0	0.0	0.0	0.0	2500.0	-1500.0	1000.0	0.0	200.0
	4	0.0	0.0	0.0	0.0	0.0	2000.0	-1500.0	500.0	0.0	1000.0
1969	1	0.0	0.0	0.0	0.0	450.0	2500.0	-1500.0	1000.0	-2200.0	500.1
	2	0.0	0.0	0.0	0.0	0.0	2500.0	-2000.0	500.0	0.0	500.1
	3	0.0	0.0	0.0	0.0	0.0	0.0	0.0	0.0	-750.0	-750.0
	4	0.0	0.0	0.0	0.0	337.5	0.0	0.0	0.0	0.0	500.0
1970	1	0.0	0.0	0.0	0.0	0.0	0.0	0.0	0.0	0.0	0.0
	2	0.0	0.0	0.0	0.0	0.0	0.0	0.0	0.0	0.0	0.0
	3	0.0	0.0	0.0	0.0	0.0	0.0	0.0	0.0	-1000.0	-662.5
	4	0.0	0.0	0.0	0.0	0.0	0.0	0.0	0.0	0.0	0.0
1971	1	0.0	800.00	0.0	0.0	0.0	0.0	0.0	0.0	0.0	800.0
	2	0.0	0.0	0.0	0.0	0.0	0.0	0.0	0.0	0.0	0.0
	3	0.0	0.0	0.0	0.0	1012.5	0.0	0.0	0.0	0.0	1012.5
	4	0.0	0.0	0.0	0.0	0.0	0.0	0.0	0.0	0.0	0.0
1972	1	0.0	0.0	0.0	0.0	0.0	0.0	0.0	0.0	0.0	0.0
	2	0.0	0.0	0.0	0.0	-320.0	0.0	0.0	0.0	0.0	-320.0

Figure 13 Page 1 of a single-run printout

PLANT EXPANSION - BRAND X. ASSUMPTIONS - NO IN/DEFLATION OF COSTS/PRICES

GRANT 20%. ANNUAL ALLOW. 25%. REDUCING BALANCE FOR 5 YEARS. CORPORATION TAX 40%

D.C.F. YIELD RATE OF RETURN = 17.9277 % PAYING RATE PER ANNUM. ACCURATE TO WITHIN 0.00001. 5.0000 % EARNING·RATE

D.C.F. NET PRESENT VALUE OF PROJECT = 1748. AT 7.0000 % PAYING & 5.0000 % EARNING RATES PER ANNUM

D.C.F. NET PRESENT VALUE OF PROJECT = 1806. AT 7.0000 % PAYING & 4.0000 % EARNING RATES PER ANNUM

D.C.F. NET PRESENT VALUE OF PROJECT = 1677. AT 8.0000 % PAYING & 4.0000 % EARNING RATES PER ANNUM

PAYBACK PERIOD ; 1 YEARS 3 PERIODS

AVERAGE ANNUAL RATE OF RETURN = 4.14 %

PRESENT VALUES OF CASH FLOWS

YEAR	PERIOD	AT 5.0000% EARNING 17.9277% PAYING PRESENT VALUE	CUMULATIVE PRESENT VALUE	AT 5.0000% EARNING 7.0000% PAYING PRESENT VALUE	CUMULATIVE PRESENT VALUE	AT 4.0000% EARNING 7.0000% PAYING PRESENT VALUE	CUMULATIVE PRESENT VALUE	AT 4.0000% EARNING 8.0000% PAYING PRESENT VALUE	CUMULATIVE PRESENT VALUE
1966	3	-10500.0	-10500.0	-10500.0	-10500.0	-10500.0	-10500.0	-10500.0	-10500.0
	4	0.0	-10500.0	0.0	-10500.0	0.0	-10500.0	0.0	-10500.0
1967	1	1381.3	-9118.7	1450.1	-9049.9	1450.1	-9049.9	1443.4	-9056.6
	2	883.7	-8235.0	950.5	-8099.4	950.5	-8099.4	943.9	-8112.7
	3	1865.6	-6369.5	2056.1	-6043.3	2056.1	-6043.3	2037.0	-6075.7
	4	1220.6	-5148.9	1378.4	-4664.9	1378.4	-4664.9	1362.4	-4713.3
1968	1	2733.0	-2415.9	3162.2	-1502.7	3162.2	-1502.7	3118.4	-1594.8
	2	749.3	-1666.5	888.3	-614.4	888.3	-614.4	874.0	-720.9
	3	143.8	-1522.7	174.7	-439.7	174.7	-439.7	171.5	-549.4
	4	690.0	-832.7	877.0	437.3	886.5	446.8	866.8	317.5
1969	1	331.7	-501.6	442.6	879.9	453.3	900.1	453.3	770.8
	2	317.1	-183.9	437.2	1317.1	448.9	1349.0	448.9	1219.6
	3	-457.3	-641.2	-647.9	669.2	-666.7	682.2	-666.7	552.9
	4	292.6	-348.7	426.7	1095.9	440.2	1122.4	440.2	993.1
1970	1	0.0	-348.7	0.0	1095.9	0.0	1122.4	0.0	993.1
	2	0.0	-348.7	0.0	1095.9	0.0	1122.4	0.0	993.1
	3	-342.5	-691.2	-545.0	550.8	-566.3	556.1	-566.3	426.7
	4	0.0	-691.2	0.0	550.8	0.0	556.1	0.0	426.7
1971	1	380.9	-310.3	642.3	1193.1	670.6	1226.6	670.6	1097.3
	2	0.0	-310.3	0.0	1193.1	0.0	1226.6	0.0	1097.3
	3	549.1	238.8	793.3	1986.5	832.2	2058.8	832.2	1929.5
	4	0.0	238.8	0.0	1986.5	0.0	2058.8	0.0	1929.5
1972	1	0.0	238.8	0.0	1986.5	0.0	2058.8	0.0	1929.5
	2	0.0	238.8	0.0	1986.5	0.0	2058.8	0.0	1929.5
	3	-238.8	-0.0	-238.8	1747.7	-252.9	1805.9	-252.9	1676.6

Figure 14 Page 2 of a single-run printout

Form 2. This contains the cash flows and year (or other period) numbers, together with certain other pieces of data, such as the 'operating year' (year in which tax depreciation begins if other than the first year) and 'tax class number' in respect of scrap values.

The cash flow cards are preceded by a Form 2 header card, and up to 30 cash flow cards (up to 60 with X4P4) are permitted in respect of every header card. The header card contains the index number (reference number), last form marker, and group index number and probability forecast for Monte Carlo runs. When only a single printout is required, a figure 1 is punched in columns 2 and 3 of the header card, the other columns being left blank.

For a single printout only one Form 2 is required. For a multiple printout up to 99 Forms 2 may be used in conjunction with each Form 1.

Form 3. Each Form 3 generates a printout, and any number of Forms 3 may be used in conjunction with each Form 1. Form 3 comprises the following:

(i) Header card, giving single run or Monte Carlo random simulation; single or dual-rate options and rates of interest; and other secondary data, including a yield accuracy stipulation (greater accuracy = longer computing time) and number of runs and other data in respect of Monte Carlo simulation, when required.

(ii) Selection card, selecting up to 40 Forms 2 for inclusion in a single run where multiple printouts giving alternative solutions are required. If random simulation is stipulated in the header card, the selection card is left blank, and the computer will automatically take into account all Forms 2 (up to 99) in the batch.

(iii) Two printout heading cards, providing 160 characters (maximum) of optional job heading which is to appear on the printout.

PROP output

This depends on whether or not a Monte Carlo exercise is required to be carried out by the computer. If so, then output in respect of the Monte Carlo run comprises a bar chart forming a probability histogram. If not, output comprises a two-page tabulated printout, page 1 giving ten cash flow tables. Page 2 gives the yield rate and NPV data, plus a further 8 tables showing NPV and cumulative NPV for each year of the project at yield solution rate and at a choice of three combinations of earning and paying rates, together with the payback period and average annual rate of return for the project. Sample printouts are illustrated in Figures 13 and 14.

Monte Carlo facility

The theory of probability is outside the scope of this book, but for those readers unfamiliar with Monte Carlo analysis a rough description follows, which it is hoped will serve to indicate what is involved by the probability facility available with the PROP system.

The probability of an event occurring can be assigned a range of values, eg, from 0 to 100, which represent the percentage probability from impossibility to certainty. If we have a *group* of alternative events, we can assign a probability percentage to each event in the group, such that the percentages add up to 100 per cent for the group.

If we now have a number of such groups (called a *batch*), the problem is to find the probability of an event occurring in the batch. To do this we allot numbers (eg, from 1 to 100) to each event within each group allocated in strict proportion to the probability percentage of each event. Selecting numbers at random we now incorporate the events corresponding to the random numbers in our calculations in order to obtain trial results. These trial results will vary at random, and can be used to build up a frequency distribution table from which a histogram or overall probability curve can be generated. This method of random number selection is referred to as the Monte Carlo method.

In the case of PROP, the computer generates random numbers during a given sample of runs over a batch of Form 2 groups to give a frequency distribution table of profitability, taking into account probability factors assigned to independent variables in the data. Thus, for example, running costs could be treated as an independent variable in this way. Probability factors could be designated to a batch of Forms 2 with varying cash flows for such costs (the other cash flows being kept constant), and by means of a Monte Carlo analysis generating random numbers over (say) 200 runs of the data, the computer could output a frequency distribution printout from which the most likely resultant yield solution rate could be read. A sample printout of a random simulation of this kind is shown in Figure 15.

The above description of the Monte Carlo facility is a very general one, intended to give only a brief indication of the way in which this facility may be used as an aid to quantifying uncertainties when analysing feasibility studies.

Conclusions

PROP is a sophisticated program, offering a comprehensive range of facilities, including advanced probability analysis. It is designed to cater extensively for the incidence of UK corporation tax and allowances, and is structured to permit multiple printouts giving alternative solutions for varying cash flows and other permutations of the data. However cash flows need to be input on individual cards in all cases of capital and revenue, and data preparation in general is rather more complex than in the case of the two less complicated systems previously described. This complexity is mitigated by the use of special coding forms obtainable from the computer manufacturers.

I.C.T. PROP

SIMULATION OF NET PRESENT VALUE FOR EXPANSION OF BRAND X

ASSUMPTION - NO COST/INCOME IN/DEFLATION, 5% GROWTH IN MARKT

NO RATE GIVEN

X · FREQUENCY AS %
* CUMULATIVE % FREQUENCY

YIELD SINGLE
SOLUTION FREQUENCY

```
34 & >   0 *
33       0 *
32       0 *
31       0 *
30       0 *
29       0 *
28       0 *
27       0 *
26       0 *
25       0 *
24       0 *
23       0 *
22       0 *
21      10 IXXXXXXXXXX*
20       0 I      **
19       0 I
18       2 IXX
17       0 I
16       0 I
15       0 I
14       0 I
13       0 I
```

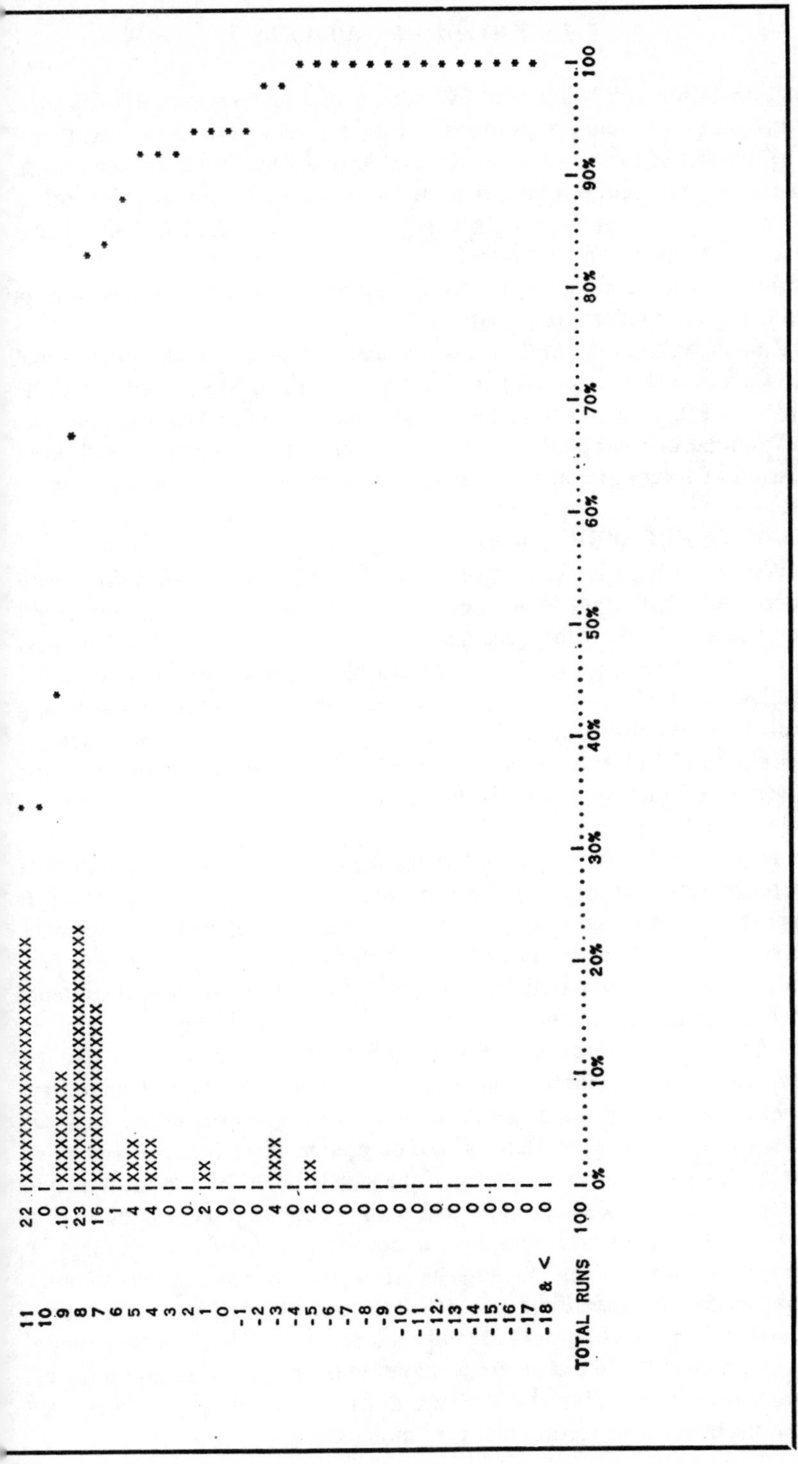

Figure 15 Yield random simulation printout and comments

THE PROSPER SYSTEM

Profit Simulation, Planning and Evaluation of Risk (PROSPER) is (like the PROP program) a system programmed for the ICL 1900 Series equipment, and may be thought of as a more advanced and flexible form of the PROP package.

To ease the problem of data preparation for such a system, special coding forms are dispensed with, and 'PROSPER flip tops' are used instead. These form a device which can be 'flipped' to the required format and slipped over the top of standard coding sheets, the flip top being changed at will according to the particular facilities required.

At time of writing, the author has not had occasion to make operational use of the PROSPER system, and no attempt at a detailed description of the system will be undertaken here. To give an indication of its facilities however, a brief outline of the system, quoted from the PROSPER manual (with kind permission of International Computers Ltd) is appended here as follows.

Outline of the PROSPER system

The 1900 Series (PROSPER) package is based on the experience gained with the successful 1900 Series PROP package. This proved that firms were ready to use computer based techniques made available in package form. The next stage was the development of a more flexible program which users could manipulate to their own particular requirements for more far-reaching analysis. It would also be desirable to arrange this program so that financial staff could handle it without assistance from programmers. In this way the effectiveness of the computer would be increased without increasing the work-load on data processing staff.

The PROSPER program in effect offers the facilities of a specialised high level computer language for cash flow forecasting, analysis and risk simulation. It consists of a range of subroutines for performing the calculations necessary for such analysis. The user controls the order in which calculations are performed, and the data required for them, by means of the order and contents of the formats he uses. There are 12 formats in all, and they represent the system bricks with which models are constructed. Each format can be represented on an 80-column punched card, or on paper tape if necessary, and controls a range of calculations for one particular aspect of the analysis. In order to reproduce a problem on the computer, therefore, the user must first break it down into calculations of the size handled by the formats and then reconstruct it as a series of format cards. The program is high level in the sense that each format operation is complete in itself and requires no further programming. The package is designed for use by accountants, financial specialists, operations research staff, etc, who can specify the series of operations required in order to obtain the desired results. The only fundamental requirements are a clear understanding of the problem, and a logical approach towards breaking the problem down into a series of format-sized calculations in order to reconstruct it in model form.

Organizing and writing down the data according to the various formats is facilitated by the use of ICL 1900 Series PROSPER flip tops (14/85) in conjunction with form 1/439 Master File Test Schedules.

In this context the term model refers not only to large scale, highly sophisticated exercises but also to any operation performed by a series of formats intended to simulate some aspect of a firm's activities. For a simple project evaluation exercise a model might consist of only twenty or so formats. The flexibility of PROSPER suits it for a variety of uses—profit forecasting and costing models, project selection, financing models, break-even analysis, etc. In most cases the real value of the computer model will prove to be the ease with which it can be updated with revised information and return at regular intervals to report progress, and the significance of changed forecasts in profit terms. Models can be amended or updated simply by punching a format, changing the sequence of formats, or by adding overwrite formats.

The basic facilities in the PROSPER package can be listed as follows:

(1) It accepts data in basic form, that is, costs, sales prices, production volume etc, and enables forecasts to be calculated as time series according to given trends and cycles if necessary.

(2) Cash flows, costs, ratios, etc, can be calculated from basic data by means of the operations provided.

(3) Special operations are provided for the calculation of investment incentives, free depreciation, loan repayment, investment income etc, with facilities for non-standard calculation if required for overseas operations etc.

(4) Special operations are provided for DCF calculations, for example, single or dual-rate calculations using constant, variable or marginal discount rates, and to given cut-off dates if required. Full printouts are automatically provided which also show discounted payback period.

(5) Risk simulation using a Monte Carlo technique for forecast selection by random numbers. Results are printed in the form of a bar chart and graph.

(6) Dependent or semi-dependent variables can be linked for selection purposes, producing greater freedom and realism in simulation models.

(7) Provision for sensitivity analysis by varying data during a given run.

(8) Optional printout of all data as it is read into the computer with listings of input errors by type and location. This gives a compact record of the model for filing and also enables the user to check the working of the model more easily.

(9) Printouts of final or intermediate results to user's requirements.

10

Select Bibliography

ALFRED, A. M. & EVANS, J. B. *Appraisal of Investment Projects by DCF*, Chapman & Hall, 1965

BOARD OF INLAND REVENUE. *Corporation Tax*, HM Stationery Office (latest edition)

BOARD OF INLAND REVENUE. *Income Tax and Corporation Tax—Capital Allowances*, leaflets C.A.1.–C.A.4. HM Stationery Office (latest editions)

BROSTER, E. J. *Appraising Capital Works*, Longman, 1968

CARR, J. L. *Investment Economics*, Routledge, 1969

CLEMENTS, R. & PARKES, D. *Manual of Maintenance 1, Building and Building Services*, Business Publications Ltd, 1965

DAVIDSON, A. W. *Parry's Valuation Tables and Conversion Tables*, Estates Gazette, 1970

DEPARTMENT OF THE ENVIRONMENT. *Costs in Use*, HM Stationery Office, 1972

DEPARTMENT OF THE ENVIRONMENT. *The Decision to Build*, HM Stationery Office, 1970

DRAKE, B. E. 'The Economics of Maintenance', *The Quantity Surveyor*, July, 1969

DEPARTMENT OF TRADE AND INDUSTRY. *New Incentives for Industry in the Assisted Areas*, DTI, 1972

FROST, M. J. *Values for Money—The Techniques of CBA*, Gower Press, 1971

INSTITUTION OF CIVIL ENGINEERS. *An Introduction to Civil Engineering Economics*, ICE, 1969

IMPERIAL CHEMICAL INDUSTRIES. *Assessing Projects—A Programme for Learning*, Methuen, 1970

INTERNATIONAL COMPUTERS LTD. *Profit Simulation, Planning and Evaluation of Risk*, ICL, 1970

INTERNATIONAL COMPUTERS LTD. *Profit Rating of Projects*, ICL, 1967

KALNITZ, M. C. *Program for Analysis of Capital Investment*, IBM, 1967

KNIGHT, H. 'Capital Cost and Cost in Use', *The Chartered Surveyor*, February, 1971

LEAN, W. & GOODALL, B. *Aspects of Land Economics*, Estates Gazette, 1966

LICHFIELD, N. *The Economics of Planned Development*, Estates Gazette, 1956

LAWSON, G. H. & WINDLE, D. W. *Tables for Discounted Cash Flow Etc*, Oliver & Boyd, 1965

MARRIOTT, O. *The Property Boom*, Hamish Hamilton, 1967

MERRETT, A. J. & SYKES, A. *Capital Budgeting and Company Finance*, Longman, 1966

MERRETT, A. J. & SYKES A. *The Finance and Analysis of Capital Projects,* Longman, 1963

MISHAN, E. J. *Cost-Benefit Analysis,* Allen & Unwin, 1971

NATIONAL ECONOMIC DEVELOPMENT COUNCIL. *Investment Appraisal,* HM Stationery Office, 1965

PAGE, C. S. & CANAWAY, E. E. *Finance for Management,* Heinemann, 1966

PILCHER, R. *Principles of Construction Management,* McGraw-Hill, 1966

ROYAL INSTITUTION OF CHARTERED SURVEYORS, *Report on the White Paper on Industrial and Regional Development,* BCIS, 1973

ROBERTSON, D. 'The Building Maintenance Cost Information Service', *The Chartered Surveyor,* February, 1972

RIX, M. S. *Investment Arithmetic,* Pitman, 1971

SOUTHWELL, J. *Total Building Cost Appraisal,* RICS, 1967

STONE, P. A. *Building Design Evaluation: Costs-in-Use,* E. & F. Spon, 1967

STONE, P. A. *Building Economy, Design, Production and Organization,* Pergamon Press, 1966

WRIGHT, M. G. *Discounted Cash Flow,* McGraw-Hill, 1967

PRESENT VALUE OF POUND.

YRS.	1	2	3	4	RATE PER CENT. 5	6	7	8	9	10	YRS.
1	0.99010	0.98039	0.97087	0.96154	0.95238	0.94340	0.93458	0.92593	0.91743	0.90909	1
2	0.98030	0.96117	0.94260	0.92456	0.90703	0.89000	0.87344	0.85734	0.84168	0.82645	2
3	0.97059	0.94232	0.91514	0.88900	0.86384	0.83962	0.81630	0.79383	0.77218	0.75131	3
4	0.96098	0.92385	0.88849	0.85480	0.82270	0.79209	0.76290	0.73503	0.70843	0.68301	4
5	0.95147	0.90573	0.86261	0.82193	0.78353	0.74726	0.71299	0.68058	0.64993	0.62092	5
6	0.94205	0.88797	0.83748	0.79031	0.74622	0.70496	0.66634	0.63017	0.59627	0.56447	6
7	0.93272	0.87056	0.81309	0.75992	0.71068	0.66506	0.62275	0.58349	0.54703	0.51316	7
8	0.92348	0.85349	0.78941	0.73069	0.67684	0.62741	0.58201	0.54027	0.50187	0.46651	8
9	0.91434	0.83676	0.76642	0.70259	0.64461	0.59190	0.54393	0.50025	0.46043	0.42410	9
10	0.90529	0.82035	0.74409	0.67556	0.61391	0.55839	0.50835	0.46319	0.42241	0.38554	10
11	0.89632	0.80426	0.72242	0.64958	0.58468	0.52679	0.47509	0.42888	0.38753	0.35049	11
12	0.88745	0.78849	0.70138	0.62460	0.55684	0.49697	0.44401	0.39711	0.35553	0.31863	12
13	0.87866	0.77303	0.68095	0.60057	0.53032	0.46884	0.41496	0.36770	0.32618	0.28966	13
14	0.86996	0.75788	0.66112	0.57748	0.50507	0.44230	0.38782	0.34046	0.29925	0.26333	14
15	0.86135	0.74301	0.64186	0.55526	0.48102	0.41727	0.36245	0.31524	0.27454	0.23939	15
16	0.85282	0.72845	0.62317	0.53391	0.45811	0.39365	0.33873	0.29189	0.25187	0.21763	16
17	0.84438	0.71416	0.60502	0.51337	0.43630	0.37136	0.31657	0.27027	0.23107	0.19784	17
18	0.83602	0.70016	0.58739	0.49363	0.41552	0.35034	0.29586	0.25025	0.21199	0.17986	18
19	0.82774	0.68643	0.57029	0.47464	0.39573	0.33051	0.27651	0.23171	0.19449	0.16351	19
20	0.81954	0.67297	0.55368	0.45639	0.37689	0.31180	0.25842	0.21455	0.17843	0.14864	20

PRESENT VALUE OF POUND.

YRS.	1	2	3	4	5	6	7	8	9	10	YRS.
					RATE PER CENT.						
21	0.81143	0.65978	0.53755	0.43883	0.35894	0.29416	0.24151	0.19866	0.16370	0.13513	21
22	0.80340	0.64684	0.52189	0.42196	0.34185	0.27751	0.22571	0.18394	0.15018	0.12285	22
23	0.79544	0.63416	0.50669	0.40573	0.32557	0.26180	0.21095	0.17032	0.13778	0.11168	23
24	0.78757	0.62172	0.49193	0.39012	0.31007	0.24698	0.19715	0.15770	0.12640	0.10153	24
25	0.77977	0.60953	0.47761	0.37512	0.29530	0.23300	0.18425	0.14602	0.11597	0.09230	25
26	0.77205	0.59758	0.46369	0.36069	0.28124	0.21981	0.17220	0.13520	0.10639	0.08391	26
27	0.76440	0.58586	0.45019	0.34682	0.26785	0.20737	0.16093	0.12519	0.09761	0.07628	27
28	0.75684	0.57437	0.43708	0.33348	0.25509	0.19563	0.15040	0.11591	0.08955	0.06934	28
29	0.74934	0.56311	0.42435	0.32065	0.24295	0.18456	0.14056	0.10733	0.08215	0.06304	29
30	0.74192	0.55207	0.41199	0.30832	0.23138	0.17411	0.13137	0.09938	0.07537	0.05731	30
31	0.73458	0.54125	0.39999	0.29646	0.22036	0.16425	0.12277	0.09202	0.06915	0.05210	31
32	0.72730	0.53063	0.38834	0.28506	0.20987	0.15496	0.11474	0.08520	0.06344	0.04736	32
33	0.72010	0.52023	0.37703	0.27409	0.19987	0.14619	0.10723	0.07889	0.05820	0.04306	33
34	0.71297	0.51003	0.36604	0.26355	0.19035	0.13791	0.10022	0.07305	0.05339	0.03914	34
35	0.70591	0.50003	0.35538	0.25342	0.18129	0.13011	0.09366	0.06763	0.04899	0.03558	35
36	0.69892	0.49022	0.34503	0.24367	0.17266	0.12274	0.08754	0.06262	0.04494	0.03235	36
37	0.69200	0.48061	0.33498	0.23430	0.16444	0.11579	0.08181	0.05799	0.04123	0.02941	37
38	0.68515	0.47119	0.32523	0.22529	0.15661	0.10924	0.07646	0.05369	0.03783	0.02673	38
39	0.67837	0.46195	0.31575	0.21662	0.14915	0.10306	0.07146	0.04971	0.03470	0.02430	39
40	0.67165	0.45289	0.30656	0.20829	0.14205	0.09722	0.06678	0.04603	0.03184	0.02209	40

PRESENT VALUE OF POUND.

YRS.	1	2	3	4	5	RATE PER CENT. 6	7	8	9	10	YRS.
41	0.66500	0.44401	0.29763	0.20028	0.13528	0.09172	0.06241	0.04262	0.02921	0.02009	41
42	0.65842	0.43530	0.28896	0.19257	0.12884	0.08653	0.05833	0.03946	0.02680	0.01826	42
43	0.65190	0.42677	0.28054	0.18517	0.12270	0.08163	0.05451	0.03654	0.02458	0.01660	43
44	0.64545	0.41840	0.27237	0.17805	0.11686	0.07701	0.05095	0.03383	0.02255	0.01509	44
45	0.63905	0.41020	0.26444	0.17120	0.11130	0.07265	0.04761	0.03133	0.02069	0.01372	45
46	0.63273	0.40215	0.25674	0.16461	0.10600	0.06854	0.04450	0.02901	0.01898	0.01247	46
47	0.62646	0.39427	0.24926	0.15828	0.10095	0.06466	0.04159	0.02686	0.01742	0.01134	47
48	0.62026	0.38654	0.24200	0.15219	0.09614	0.06100	0.03887	0.02487	0.01598	0.01031	48
49	0.61412	0.37896	0.23495	0.14634	0.09156	0.05755	0.03632	0.02303	0.01466	0.00937	49
50	0.60804	0.37153	0.22811	0.14071	0.08720	0.05429	0.03395	0.02132	0.01345	0.00852	50
51	0.60202	0.36424	0.22146	0.13530	0.08305	0.05122	0.03173	0.01974	0.01234	0.00774	51
52	0.59606	0.35710	0.21501	0.13010	0.07910	0.04832	0.02965	0.01828	0.01132	0.00704	52
53	0.59016	0.35010	0.20875	0.12509	0.07533	0.04558	0.02771	0.01693	0.01038	0.00640	53
54	0.58431	0.34323	0.20267	0.12028	0.07174	0.04300	0.02590	0.01567	0.00953	0.00582	54
55	0.57853	0.33650	0.19677	0.11566	0.06833	0.04057	0.02420	0.01451	0.00874	0.00529	55
56	0.57280	0.32991	0.19104	0.11121	0.06507	0.03827	0.02262	0.01344	0.00802	0.00481	56
57	0.56713	0.32344	0.18547	0.10693	0.06197	0.03610	0.02114	0.01244	0.00736	0.00437	57
58	0.56151	0.31710	0.18007	0.10282	0.05902	0.03406	0.01976	0.01152	0.00675	0.00397	58
59	0.55595	0.31088	0.17483	0.09886	0.05621	0.03213	0.01847	0.01067	0.00619	0.00361	59
60	0.55045	0.30478	0.16973	0.09506	0.05354	0.03031	0.01726	0.00988	0.00568	0.00328	60

PRESENT VALUE OF POUND.

YRS.	11	12	13	14	RATE PER CENT. 15.	16	17	18	19	20	YRS.
1	0.90090	0.89286	0.88496	0.87719	0.86957	0.86207	0.85470	0.84746	0.84034	0.83333	1
2	0.81162	0.79719	0.78315	0.76947	0.75614	0.74316	0.73051	0.71818	0.70616	0.69444	2
3	0.73119	0.71178	0.69305	0.67497	0.65752	0.64066	0.62437	0.60863	0.59342	0.57870	3
4	0.65873	0.63552	0.61332	0.59208	0.57175	0.55229	0.53365	0.51579	0.49867	0.48225	4
5	0.59345	0.56743	0.54276	0.51937	0.49718	0.47611	0.45611	0.43711	0.41905	0.40188	5
6	0.53464	0.50663	0.48032	0.45559	0.43233	0.41044	0.38984	0.37043	0.35214	0.33490	6
7	0.48166	0.45235	0.42506	0.39964	0.37594	0.35383	0.33320	0.31393	0.29592	0.27908	7
8	0.43393	0.40388	0.37616	0.35056	0.32690	0.30503	0.28478	0.26604	0.24867	0.23257	8
9	0.39092	0.36061	0.33288	0.30751	0.28426	0.26295	0.24340	0.22546	0.20897	0.19381	9
10	0.35218	0.32197	0.29459	0.26974	0.24718	0.22668	0.20804	0.19106	0.17560	0.16151	10
11	0.31728	0.28748	0.26070	0.23662	0.21494	0.19542	0.17781	0.16192	0.14757	0.13459	11
12	0.28584	0.25668	0.23071	0.20756	0.18691	0.16846	0.15197	0.13722	0.12400	0.11216	12
13	0.25751	0.22917	0.20416	0.18207	0.16253	0.14523	0.12989	0.11629	0.10421	0.09346	13
14	0.23199	0.20462	0.18068	0.15971	0.14133	0.12520	0.11102	0.09855	0.08757	0.07789	14
15	0.20900	0.18270	0.15989	0.14010	0.12289	0.10793	0.09489	0.08352	0.07359	0.06491	15
16	0.18829	0.16312	0.14150	0.12289	0.10686	0.09304	0.08110	0.07078	0.06184	0.05409	16
17	0.16963	0.14564	0.12522	0.10780	0.09293	0.08021	0.06932	0.05998	0.05196	0.04507	17
18	0.15282	0.13004	0.11081	0.09456	0.08081	0.06914	0.05925	0.05083	0.04367	0.03756	18
19	0.13768	0.11611	0.09806	0.08295	0.07027	0.05961	0.05064	0.04308	0.03670	0.03130	19
20	0.12403	0.10367	0.08678	0.07276	0.06110	0.05139	0.04328	0.03651	0.03084	0.02608	20

Construction cost appraisal

PRESENT VALUE OF POUND.

RATE PER CENT.

YRS.	20	19	18	17	16	15	14	13	12	11	YRS.
21	0.02174	0.02591	0.03094	0.03699	0.04430	0.05213	0.06383	0.07680	0.09256	0.11174	21
22	0.01811	0.02178	0.02622	0.03162	0.03819	0.04620	0.05599	0.06796	0.08264	0.10067	22
23	0.01509	0.01830	0.02222	0.02702	0.03292	0.04017	0.04911	0.06014	0.07379	0.09069	23
24	0.01258	0.01538	0.01883	0.02310	0.02838	0.03493	0.04308	0.05323	0.06588	0.08170	24
25	0.01048	0.01292	0.01596	0.01974	0.02447	0.03038	0.03779	0.04710	0.05882	0.07361	25
26	0.00874	0.01086	0.01352	0.01687	0.02109	0.02642	0.03315	0.04168	0.05252	0.06631	26
27	0.00728	0.00912	0.01146	0.01442	0.01818	0.02297	0.02908	0.03689	0.04689	0.05974	27
28	0.00607	0.00767	0.00971	0.01233	0.01567	0.01997	0.02551	0.03264	0.04187	0.05382	28
29	0.00506	0.00644	0.00823	0.01053	0.01351	0.01737	0.02237	0.02889	0.03738	0.04849	29
30	0.00421	0.00541	0.00697	0.00900	0.01165	0.01510	0.01963	0.02557	0.03338	0.04368	30
31	0.00351	0.00455	0.00591	0.00770	0.01004	0.01313	0.01722	0.02262	0.02980	0.03935	31
32	0.00293	0.00382	0.00501	0.00658	0.00866	0.01142	0.01510	0.02002	0.02661	0.03545	32
33	0.00244	0.00321	0.00425	0.00562	0.00746	0.00993	0.01325	0.01772	0.02376	0.03194	33
34	0.00203	0.00270	0.00360	0.00480	0.00643	0.00864	0.01162	0.01568	0.02121	0.02878	34
35	0.00169	0.00227	0.00305	0.00411	0.00555	0.00751	0.01019	0.01388	0.01894	0.02592	35
36	0.00141	0.00191	0.00258	0.00351	0.00478	0.00653	0.00894	0.01228	0.01691	0.02335	36
37	0.00118	0.00160	0.00219	0.00300	0.00412	0.00568	0.00784	0.01087	0.01510	0.02104	37
38	0.00098	0.00135	0.00186	0.00256	0.00355	0.00494	0.00688	0.00962	0.01348	0.01896	38
39	0.00082	0.00113	0.00157	0.00219	0.00306	0.00429	0.00604	0.00851	0.01204	0.01708	39
40	0.00068	0.00095	0.00133	0.00187	0.00264	0.00373	0.00529	0.00753	0.01075	0.01538	40

YRS.	30	29	28	27	RATE PER CENT. 26	25	24	23	22	21	YRS.
1	0.76923	0.77519	0.78125	0.78740	0.79365	0.80000	0.80645	0.81301	0.81967	0.82645	1
2	0.59172	0.60093	0.61035	0.62000	0.62988	0.64000	0.65036	0.66098	0.67186	0.68301	2
3	0.45517	0.46583	0.47684	0.48819	0.49991	0.51200	0.52449	0.53738	0.55071	0.56447	3
4	0.35013	0.36111	0.37253	0.38440	0.39675	0.40960	0.42297	0.43690	0.45140	0.46651	4
5	0.26933	0.27993	0.29104	0.30268	0.31488	0.32768	0.34111	0.35520	0.37000	0.38554	5
6	0.20718	0.21700	0.22737	0.23833	0.24991	0.26214	0.27509	0.28878	0.30328	0.31863	6
7	0.15937	0.16822	0.17764	0.18766	0.19834	0.20972	0.22184	0.23478	0.24859	0.26333	7
8	0.12259	0.13040	0.13878	0.14776	0.15741	0.16777	0.17891	0.19088	0.20376	0.21763	8
9	0.09430	0.10109	0.10842	0.11635	0.12493	0.13422	0.14428	0.15519	0.16702	0.17986	9
10	0.07254	0.07836	0.08470	0.09161	0.09915	0.10737	0.11635	0.12617	0.13690	0.14864	10
11	0.05580	0.06075	0.06617	0.07214	0.07869	0.08590	0.09383	0.10258	0.11221	0.12285	11
12	0.04292	0.04709	0.05170	0.05680	0.06245	0.06872	0.07567	0.08339	0.09198	0.10153	12
13	0.03302	0.03650	0.04039	0.04473	0.04957	0.05498	0.06103	0.06780	0.07539	0.08391	13
14	0.02540	0.02830	0.03155	0.03522	0.03934	0.04398	0.04921	0.05512	0.06180	0.06934	14
15	0.01954	0.02194	0.02465	0.02773	0.03122	0.03518	0.03969	0.04481	0.05065	0.05731	15
16	0.01503	0.01700	0.01926	0.02183	0.02478	0.02815	0.03201	0.03643	0.04152	0.04736	16
17	0.01156	0.01318	0.01505	0.01719	0.01967	0.02252	0.02581	0.02962	0.03403	0.03914	17
18	0.00889	0.01022	0.01175	0.01354	0.01561	0.01801	0.02082	0.02408	0.02789	0.03235	18
19	0.00684	0.00792	0.00918	0.01066	0.01239	0.01441	0.01679	0.01958	0.02286	0.02673	19
20	0.00526	0.00614	0.00717	0.00839	0.00983	0.01153	0.01354	0.01592	0.01874	0.02209	20

PRESENT VALUE OF POUND.

YRS.	RATE PER CENT. 21	22	23	24	25	26	27	28	29	30	YRS.
21	0.01826	0.01536	0.01294	0.01092	0.00922	0.00780	0.00661	0.00561	0.00476	0.00405	21
22	0.01509	0.01259	0.01052	0.00880	0.00738	0.00619	0.00520	0.00438	0.00369	0.00311	22
23	0.01247	0.01032	0.00855	0.00710	0.00590	0.00491	0.00410	0.00342	0.00286	0.00239	23
24	0.01031	0.00846	0.00695	0.00573	0.00472	0.00390	0.00323	0.00267	0.00222	0.00184	24
25	0.00852	0.00693	0.00565	0.00462	0.00378	0.00310	0.00254	0.00209	0.00172	0.00142	25
26	0.00704	0.00568	0.00460	0.00372	0.00302	0.00246	0.00200	0.00163	0.00133	0.00109	26
27	0.00582	0.00466	0.00374	0.00300	0.00242	0.00195	0.00158	0.00127	0.00103	0.00084	27
28	0.00481	0.00382	0.00304	0.00242	0.00193	0.00155	0.00124	0.00100	0.00080	0.00065	28
29	0.00397	0.00313	0.00247	0.00195	0.00155	0.00123	0.00098	0.00078	0.00062	0.00050	29
30	0.00328	0.00257	0.00201	0.00158	0.00124	0.00097	0.00077	0.00061	0.00048	0.00038	30
31	0.00271	0.00210	0.00163	0.00127	0.00099	0.00077	0.00061	0.00047	0.00037	0.00029	31
32	0.00224	0.00172	0.00133	0.00102	0.00079	0.00061	0.00048	0.00037	0.00029	0.00023	32
33	0.00185	0.00141	0.00108	0.00083	0.00063	0.00049	0.00038	0.00029	0.00022	0.00017	33
34	0.00153	0.00116	0.00088	0.00067	0.00051	0.00039	0.00030	0.00023	0.00017	0.00013	34
35	0.00127	0.00095	0.00071	0.00054	0.00041	0.00031	0.00023	0.00018	0.00013	0.00010	35
36	0.00105	0.00078	0.00058	0.00043	0.00032	0.00024	0.00018	0.00014	0.00010	0.00008	36
37	0.00086	0.00064	0.00047	0.00035	0.00026	0.00019	0.00014	0.00011	0.00008	0.00006	37
38	0.00071	0.00052	0.00038	0.00028	0.00021	0.00015	0.00011	0.00008	0.00006	0.00005	38
39	0.00059	0.00043	0.00031	0.00023	0.00017	0.00012	0.00009	0.00007	0.00005	0.00004	39
40	0.00049	0.00035	0.00025	0.00018	0.00013	0.00010	0.00007	0.00005	0.00004	0.00003	40

PRESENT VALUE OF POUND PER ANNUM. (SINGLE RATE YEARS PURCHASE.)

YRS.	RATE PER CENT. 1	2	3	4	5	6	7	8	9	10
1	0.9901	0.9804	0.9709	0.9615	0.9524	0.9434	0.9346	0.9259	0.9174	0.9091
2	1.9704	1.9416	1.9135	1.8861	1.8594	1.8334	1.8080	1.7833	1.7591	1.7355
3	2.9410	2.8839	2.8286	2.7751	2.7232	2.6730	2.6243	2.5771	2.5313	2.4869
4	3.9020	3.8077	3.7171	3.6299	3.5460	3.4651	3.3872	3.3121	3.2397	3.1699
5	4.8534	4.7135	4.5797	4.4518	4.3295	4.2124	4.1002	3.9927	3.8897	3.7908
6	5.7955	5.6014	5.4172	5.2421	5.0757	4.9173	4.7665	4.6229	4.4859	4.3553
7	6.7282	6.4720	6.2303	6.0021	5.7864	5.5824	5.3893	5.2064	5.0330	4.8684
8	7.6517	7.3255	7.0197	6.7327	6.4632	6.2098	5.9713	5.7466	5.5348	5.3349
9	8.5660	8.1622	7.7861	7.4353	7.1078	6.8017	6.5152	6.2469	5.9952	5.7590
10	9.4713	8.9826	8.5302	8.1109	7.7217	7.3601	7.0236	6.7101	6.4177	6.1446
11	10.3676	9.7868	9.2526	8.7605	8.3064	7.8869	7.4987	7.1390	6.8052	6.4951
12	11.2551	10.5753	9.9540	9.3851	8.8633	8.3838	7.9427	7.5361	7.1607	6.8137
13	12.1337	11.3484	10.6350	9.9856	9.3936	8.8527	8.3577	7.9038	7.4869	7.1034
14	13.0037	12.1062	11.2961	10.5631	9.8986	9.2950	8.7455	8.2442	7.7862	7.3667
15	13.8651	12.8493	11.9379	11.1184	10.3797	9.7122	9.1079	8.5595	8.0607	7.6061
16	14.7179	13.5777	12.5611	11.6523	10.8378	10.1059	9.4466	8.8514	8.3126	7.8237
17	15.5623	14.2919	13.1661	12.1657	11.2741	10.4773	9.7632	9.1216	8.5436	8.0216
18	16.3983	14.9920	13.7535	12.6593	11.6896	10.8276	10.0591	9.3719	8.7556	8.2014
19	17.2260	15.6785	14.3238	13.1339	12.0853	11.1581	10.3356	9.6036	8.9501	8.3649
20	18.0456	16.3514	14.8775	13.5903	12.4622	11.4699	10.5940	9.8181	9.1285	8.5136

PRESENT VALUE OF POUND PER ANNUM. (SINGLE RATE YEARS PURCHASE.)

YRS.	1	2	3	4	5	6	7	8	9	10	YRS.
21	18.8570	17.0112	15.4150	14.0292	12.8212	11.7641	10.8355	10.0168	9.2922	8.6487	21
22	19.6604	17.6580	15.9369	14.4511	13.1630	12.0416	11.0612	10.2007	9.4424	8.7715	22
23	20.4558	18.2922	16.4436	14.8568	13.4886	12.3034	11.2722	10.3711	9.5802	8.8832	23
24	21.2434	18.9139	16.9355	15.2470	13.7986	12.5504	11.4693	10.5288	9.7066	8.9847	24
25	22.0232	19.5235	17.4131	15.6221	14.0939	12.7834	11.6536	10.6748	9.8226	9.0770	25
26	22.7952	20.1210	17.8768	15.9828	14.3752	13.0032	11.8258	10.8100	9.9290	9.1609	26
27	23.5596	20.7069	18.3270	16.3296	14.6430	13.2105	11.9867	10.9352	10.0266	9.2372	27
28	24.3164	21.2813	18.7641	16.6631	14.8981	13.4062	12.1371	11.0511	10.1161	9.3066	28
29	25.0658	21.8444	19.1885	16.9837	15.1411	13.5907	12.2777	11.1584	10.1983	9.3696	29
30	25.8077	22.3965	19.6004	17.2920	15.3725	13.7648	12.4090	11.2578	10.2737	9.4269	30
31	26.5423	22.9377	20.0004	17.5885	15.5928	13.9291	12.5318	11.3498	10.3428	9.4790	31
32	27.2696	23.4683	20.3888	17.8736	15.8027	14.0840	12.6466	11.4350	10.4062	9.5264	32
33	27.9897	23.9886	20.7658	18.1476	16.0025	14.2302	12.7538	11.5139	10.4644	9.5694	33
34	28.7027	24.4986	21.1318	18.4112	16.1929	14.3681	12.8540	11.5869	10.5178	9.6086	34
35	29.4086	24.9986	21.4872	18.6646	16.3742	14.4982	12.9477	11.6546	10.5668	9.6442	35
36	30.1075	25.4888	21.8323	18.9083	16.5469	14.6210	13.0352	11.7172	10.6118	9.6765	36
37	30.7995	25.9695	22.1672	19.1426	16.7113	14.7368	13.1170	11.7752	10.6530	9.7059	37
38	31.4847	26.4406	22.4925	19.3679	16.8679	14.8460	13.1935	11.8289	10.6908	9.7327	38
39	32.1630	26.9026	22.8082	19.5845	17.0170	14.9491	13.2649	11.8786	10.7255	9.7570	39
40	32.8347	27.3555	23.1148	19.7928	17.1591	15.0463	13.3317	11.9246	10.7574	9.7791	40

RATE PER CENT.

PRESENT VALUE OF POUND PER ANNUM (SINGLE RATE YEARS PURCHASE)

YRS.	1	2	3	4	RATE PER CENT. 5	6	7	8	9	10	YRS.
41	33.4997	27.7995	23.4124	19.9931	17.2944	15.1380	13.3941	11.9672	10.7866	9.7991	41
42	34.1581	28.2348	23.7014	20.1856	17.4232	15.2245	13.4524	12.0067	10.8134	9.8174	42
43	34.8100	28.6616	23.9819	20.3708	17.5459	15.3062	13.5070	12.0432	10.8380	9.8340	43
44	35.4555	29.0800	24.2543	20.5488	17.6628	15.3832	13.5579	12.0771	10.8605	9.8491	44
45	36.0945	29.4902	24.5187	20.7200	17.7741	15.4558	13.6055	12.1084	10.8812	9.8628	45
46	36.7272	29.8923	24.7754	20.8847	17.8801	15.5244	13.6500	12.1374	10.9002	9.8753	46
47	37.3537	30.2866	25.0247	21.0429	17.9810	15.5890	13.6916	12.1643	10.9176	9.8866	47
48	37.9740	30.6731	25.2667	21.1951	18.0772	15.6500	13.7305	12.1891	10.9336	9.8969	48
49	38.5881	31.0521	25.5017	21.3415	18.1687	15.7076	13.7668	12.2122	10.9482	9.9063	49
50	39.1961	31.4236	25.7298	21.4822	18.2559	15.7619	13.8007	12.2335	10.9617	9.9148	50
51	39.7981	31.7878	25.9512	21.6175	18.3390	15.8131	13.8325	12.2532	10.9740	9.9226	51
52	40.3942	32.1449	26.1662	21.7476	18.4181	15.8614	13.8621	12.2715	10.9853	9.9296	52
53	40.9843	32.4950	26.3750	21.8727	18.4934	15.9070	13.8898	12.2884	10.9957	9.9360	53
54	41.5687	32.8383	26.5777	21.9930	18.5651	15.9500	13.9157	12.3041	11.0053	9.9418	54
55	42.1472	33.1748	26.7744	22.1086	18.6335	15.9905	13.9399	12.3186	11.0140	9.9471	55
56	42.7200	33.5047	26.9655	22.2198	18.6985	16.0288	13.9626	12.3321	11.0220	9.9519	56
57	43.2871	33.8281	27.1509	22.3267	18.7605	16.0649	13.9837	12.3445	11.0294	9.9563	57
58	43.8486	34.1452	27.3310	22.4296	18.8195	16.0990	14.0035	12.3560	11.0361	9.9603	58
59	44.4046	34.4561	27.5058	22.5284	18.8758	16.1311	14.0219	12.3667	11.0423	9.9639	59
60	44.9550	34.7609	27.6756	22.6235	18.9293	16.1614	14.0392	12.3766	11.0480	9.9672	60

PRESENT VALUE OF POUND PER ANNUM. (SINGLE RATE YEARS PURCHASE.)

YRS.	RATE PER CENT.										YRS.
	11	12	13	14	15	16	17	18	19	20	
1	0.9009	0.8929	0.8850	0.8772	0.8696	0.8621	0.8547	0.8475	0.8403	0.8333	1
2	1.7125	1.6901	1.6681	1.6467	1.6257	1.6052	1.5852	1.5656	1.5465	1.5278	2
3	2.4437	2.4018	2.3612	2.3216	2.2832	2.2459	2.2096	2.1743	2.1399	2.1065	3
4	3.1024	3.0373	2.9745	2.9137	2.8550	2.7982	2.7432	2.6901	2.6386	2.5887	4
5	3.6959	3.6048	3.5172	3.4331	3.3522	3.2743	3.1993	3.1272	3.0576	2.9906	5
6	4.2305	4.1114	3.9975	3.8887	3.7845	3.6847	3.5892	3.4976	3.4098	3.3255	6
7	4.7122	4.5638	4.4226	4.2883	4.1604	4.0386	3.9224	3.8115	3.7057	3.6046	7
8	5.1461	4.9676	4.7988	4.6389	4.4873	4.3436	4.2072	4.0776	3.9544	3.8372	8
9	5.5370	5.3282	5.1317	4.9464	4.7716	4.6065	4.4506	4.3030	4.1633	4.0310	9
10	5.8892	5.6502	5.4262	5.2161	5.0188	4.8332	4.6586	4.4941	4.3389	4.1925	10
11	6.2065	5.9377	5.6869	5.4527	5.2337	5.0286	4.8364	4.6560	4.4865	4.3271	11
12	6.4924	6.1944	5.9176	5.6603	5.4206	5.1971	4.9884	4.7932	4.6105	4.4392	12
13	6.7499	6.4235	6.1218	5.8424	5.5831	5.3423	5.1183	4.9095	4.7147	4.5327	13
14	6.9819	6.6282	6.3025	6.0021	5.7245	5.4675	5.2293	5.0081	4.8023	4.6106	14
15	7.1909	6.8109	6.4624	6.1422	5.8474	5.5755	5.3242	5.0916	4.8759	4.6755	15
16	7.3792	6.9740	6.6039	6.2651	5.9542	5.6685	5.4053	5.1624	4.9377	4.7296	16
17	7.5488	7.1196	6.7291	6.3729	6.0472	5.7487	5.4746	5.2223	4.9897	4.7746	17
18	7.7016	7.2497	6.8399	6.4074	6.1280	5.8178	5.5339	5.2732	5.0333	4.8122	18
19	7.8393	7.3658	6.9380	6.5504	6.1982	5.8775	5.5845	5.3162	5.0700	4.8435	19
20	7.9633	7.4694	7.0248	6.6231	6.2593	5.9288	5.6278	5.3527	5.1009	4.8696	20

PRESENT VALUE OF POUND PER ANNUM. (SINGLE RATE YEARS PURCHASE.)

YRS.	11	12	13	14	RATE PER CENT. 15	16	17	18	19	20	YRS.
21	8.0751	7.5620	7.1016	6.6870	6.3125	5.9731	5.6648	5.3837	5.1268	4.8913	21
22	8.1757	7.6446	7.1695	6.7429	6.3587	6.0113	5.6964	5.4099	5.1486	4.9094	22
23	8.2664	7.7184	7.2297	6.7921	6.3988	6.0442	5.7234	5.4321	5.1668	4.9245	23
24	8.3481	7.7843	7.2829	6.8351	6.4338	6.0726	5.7465	5.4509	5.1822	4.9371	24
25	8.4217	7.8431	7.3300	6.8729	6.4641	6.0971	5.7662	5.4669	5.1951	4.9476	25
26	8.4881	7.8957	7.3717	6.9061	6.4906	6.1182	5.7831	5.4804	5.2060	4.9563	26
27	8.5478	7.9426	7.4086	6.9352	6.5135	6.1364	5.7975	5.4919	5.2151	4.9636	27
28	8.6016	7.9844	7.4412	6.9607	6.5335	6.1520	5.8099	5.5016	5.2228	4.9697	28
29	8.6501	8.0218	7.4701	6.9830	6.5509	6.1656	5.8204	5.5098	5.2292	4.9747	29
30	8.6938	8.0552	7.4957	7.0027	6.5660	6.1772	5.8294	5.5168	5.2347	4.9789	30
31	8.7331	8.0850	7.5183	7.0199	6.5791	6.1872	5.8371	5.5227	5.2392	4.9824	31
32	8.7686	8.1116	7.5383	7.0350	6.5905	6.1959	5.8437	5.5277	5.2430	4.9854	32
33	8.8005	8.1354	7.5560	7.0482	6.6005	6.2034	5.8493	5.5320	5.2462	4.9878	33
34	8.8293	8.1566	7.5717	7.0599	6.6091	6.2098	5.8541	5.5356	5.2489	4.9898	34
35	8.8552	8.1755	7.5856	7.0700	6.6166	6.2153	5.8582	5.5386	5.2512	4.9915	35
36	8.8786	8.1924	7.5979	7.0790	6.6231	6.2201	5.8617	5.5412	5.2531	4.9929	36
37	8.8996	8.2075	7.6087	7.0868	6.6288	6.2242	5.8647	5.5434	5.2547	4.9941	37
38	8.9186	8.2210	7.6183	7.0937	6.6338	6.2278	5.8673	5.5452	5.2561	4.9951	38
39	8.9357	8.2330	7.6268	7.0997	6.6380	6.2309	5.8695	5.5468	5.2572	4.9959	39
40	8.9511	8.2438	7.6344	7.1050	6.6418	6.2335	5.8713	5.5482	5.2582	4.9966	40

PRESENT VALUE OF POUND PER ANNUM. (SINGLE RATE YEARS PURCHASE.)

YRS.	11	12	13	14	RATE PER CENT. 15	16	17	18	19	20	YRS.
41	8.9649	8.2534	7.6410	7.1097	6.6450	6.2358	5.8729	5.5493	5.2590	4.9972	41
42	8.9774	8.2619	7.6469	7.1138	6.6478	6.2377	5.8743	5.5502	5.2596	4.9976	42
43	8.9886	8.2696	7.6522	7.1173	6.6503	6.2394	5.8755	5.5510	5.2602	4.9980	43
44	8.9988	8.2764	7.6568	7.1205	6.6524	6.2409	5.8765	5.5517	5.2607	4.9984	44
45	9.0079	8.2825	7.6609	7.1232	6.6543	6.2421	5.8773	5.5523	5.2611	4.9986	45
46	9.0161	8.2880	7.6645	7.1256	6.6559	6.2432	5.8781	5.5528	5.2614	4.9989	46
47	9.0235	8.2928	7.6677	7.1277	6.6573	6.2442	5.8787	5.5532	5.2617	4.9991	47
48	9.0302	8.2972	7.6705	7.1296	6.6585	6.2450	5.8792	5.5536	5.2619	4.9992	48
49	9.0362	8.3010	7.6730	7.1312	6.6596	6.2457	5.8797	5.5539	5.2621	4.9993	49
50	9.0417	8.3045	7.6752	7.1327	6.6605	6.2463	5.8801	5.5541	5.2623	4.9995	50
51	9.0465	8.3076	7.6772	7.1339	6.6613	6.2468	5.8804	5.5544	5.2624	4.9995	51
52	9.0509	8.3103	7.6789	7.1350	6.6620	6.2472	5.8807	5.5545	5.2625	4.9996	52
53	9.0549	8.3128	7.6805	7.1360	6.6626	6.2476	5.8809	5.5547	5.2626	4.9997	53
54	9.0585	8.3150	7.6818	7.1368	6.6631	6.2479	5.8811	5.5548	5.2627	4.9997	54
55	9.0617	8.3170	7.6830	7.1376	6.6636	6.2482	5.8813	5.5549	5.2628	4.9998	55
56	9.0646	8.3187	7.6841	7.1382	6.6640	6.2485	5.8815	5.5550	5.2628	4.9998	56
57	9.0672	8.3203	7.6851	7.1388	6.6644	6.2487	5.8816	5.5551	5.2629	4.9998	57
58	9.0695	8.3217	7.6859	7.1393	6.6647	6.2489	5.8817	5.5552	5.2629	4.9999	58
59	9.0717	8.3229	7.6866	7.1397	6.6649	6.2490	5.8818	5.5552	5.2630	4.9999	59
60	9.0736	8.3240	7.6873	7.1401	6.6651	6.2492	5.8819	5.5553	5.2630	4.9999	60

PRESENT VALUE.OF POUND PER ANNUM. (SINGLE RATE YEARS PURCHASE.)

RATE PER CENT.

YRS.	21	22	23	24	25	26	27	28	29	30	YRS.
1	0.8264	0.8197	0.8130	0.8065	0.8000	0.7937	0.7874	0.7813	0.7752	0.7692	1
2	1.5095	1.4915	1.4740	1.4568	1.4400	1.4235	1.4074	1.3916	1.3761	1.3609	2
3	2.0739	2.0422	2.0114	1.9813	1.9520	1.9234	1.8956	1.8684	1.8420	1.8161	3
4	2.5404	2.4936	2.4483	2.4043	2.3616	2.3202	2.2800	2.2410	2.2031	2.1662	4
5	2.9260	2.8636	2.8035	2.7454	2.6893	2.6351	2.5827	2.5320	2.4830	2.4356	5
6	3.2446	3.1669	3.0923	3.0205	2.9514	2.8850	2.8210	2.7594	2.7000	2.6427	6
7	3.5079	3.4155	3.3270	3.2423	3.1611	3.0833	3.0087	2.9370	2.8682	2.8021	7
8	3.7256	3.6193	3.5179	3.4212	3.3289	3.2407	3.1564	3.0758	2.9986	2.9247	8
9	3.9054	3.7863	3.6731	3.5655	3.4631	3.3657	3.2728	3.1842	3.0997	3.0190	9
10	4.0541	3.9232	3.7993	3.6819	3.5705	3.4648	3.3644	3.2689	3.1781	3.0915	10
11	4.1769	4.0354	3.9018	3.7757	3.6564	3.5435	3.4365	3.3351	3.2386	3.1473	11
12	4.2784	4.1274	3.9852	3.8514	3.7251	3.6059	3.4933	3.3868	3.2859	3.1903	12
13	4.3624	4.2028	4.0530	3.9124	3.7801	3.6555	3.5381	3.4272	3.3224	3.2233	13
14	4.4317	4.2646	4.1082	3.9616	3.8241	3.6949	3.5733	3.4587	3.3507	3.2487	14
15	4.4890	4.3152	4.1530	4.0013	3.8593	3.7261	3.6010	3.4834	3.3726	3.2682	15
16	4.5364	4.3567	4.1894	4.0333	3.8874	3.7509	3.6228	3.5026	3.3896	3.2832	16
17	4.5755	4.3908	4.2190	4.0591	3.9099	3.7705	3.6400	3.5177	3.4028	3.2948	17
18	4.6079	4.4187	4.2431	4.0799	3.9279	3.7861	3.6536	3.5294	3.4130	3.3037	18
19	4.6346	4.4415	4.2627	4.0967	3.9424	3.7985	3.6642	3.5386	3.4210	3.3105	19
20	4.6567	4.4603	4.2786	4.1103	3.9539	3.8083	3.6726	3.5458	3.4271	3.3158	20

ANNUAL SINKING FUND.

YRS.	0.25	0.50	0.75	1.00	1.25	1.50	1.75	2.00	2.25	2.50
1	1.00000	1.00000	1.00000	1.00000	1.00000	1.00000	1.00000	1.00000	1.00000	1.00000
2	0.49938	0.49875	0.49813	0.49751	0.49689	0.49628	0.49566	0.49505	0.49444	0.49383
3	0.33250	0.33167	0.33085	0.33002	0.32920	0.32838	0.32757	0.32675	0.32594	0.32514
4	0.24906	0.24813	0.24721	0.24628	0.24536	0.24444	0.24353	0.24262	0.24172	0.24082
5	0.19900	0.19801	0.19702	0.19604	0.19506	0.19409	0.19312	0.19216	0.19120	0.19025
6	0.16563	0.16460	0.16357	0.16255	0.16153	0.16053	0.15952	0.15853	0.15753	0.15655
7	0.14179	0.14073	0.13967	0.13863	0.13759	0.13656	0.13553	0.13451	0.13350	0.13250
8	0.12391	0.12283	0.12176	0.12069	0.11963	0.11858	0.11754	0.11651	0.11548	0.11447
9	0.11000	0.10891	0.10782	0.10674	0.10567	0.10461	0.10356	0.10252	0.10148	0.10046
10	0.09888	0.09777	0.09667	0.09558	0.09450	0.09343	0.09238	0.09133	0.09029	0.08926
11	0.08978	0.08866	0.08755	0.08645	0.08537	0.08429	0.08323	0.08218	0.08114	0.08011
12	0.08219	0.08107	0.07995	0.07885	0.07776	0.07668	0.07561	0.07456	0.07352	0.07249
13	0.07578	0.07464	0.07352	0.07241	0.07132	0.07024	0.06917	0.06812	0.06708	0.06605
14	0.07028	0.06914	0.06801	0.06690	0.06581	0.06472	0.06366	0.06260	0.06156	0.06054
15	0.06551	0.06436	0.06324	0.06212	0.06103	0.05994	0.05888	0.05783	0.05679	0.05577
16	0.06134	0.06019	0.05906	0.05794	0.05685	0.05577	0.05470	0.05365	0.05262	0.05160
17	0.05766	0.05651	0.05537	0.05426	0.05316	0.05208	0.05102	0.04997	0.04894	0.04793
18	0.05438	0.05323	0.05210	0.05098	0.04988	0.04881	0.04774	0.04670	0.04568	0.04467
19	0.05146	0.05030	0.04917	0.04805	0.04696	0.04588	0.04482	0.04378	0.04276	0.04176
20	0.04882	0.04767	0.04653	0.04542	0.04432	0.04325	0.04219	0.04116	0.04014	0.03930

ANNUAL SINKING FUND.

YRS.	0.25	0.50	0.75	1.00	1.25	RATE PER CENT. 1.50	1.75	2.00	2.25	2.50	YRS.
21	0.04644	0.04528	0.04415	0.04303	0.04194	0.04087	0.03981	0.03878	0.03778	0.03679	21
22	0.04427	0.04311	0.04198	0.04086	0.03977	0.03870	0.03766	0.03663	0.03563	0.03465	22
23	0.04229	0.04113	0.04000	0.03889	0.03780	0.03673	0.03569	0.03467	0.03367	0.03270	23
24	0.04048	0.03932	0.03818	0.03707	0.03599	0.03492	0.03389	0.03287	0.03188	0.03091	24
25	0.03881	0.03765	0.03652	0.03541	0.03432	0.03326	0.03223	0.03122	0.03024	0.02928	25
26	0.03727	0.03611	0.03498	0.03387	0.03279	0.03173	0.03070	0.02970	0.02872	0.02777	26
27	0.03585	0.03469	0.03355	0.03245	0.03137	0.03032	0.02929	0.02829	0.02732	0.02638	27
28	0.03452	0.03336	0.03223	0.03112	0.03005	0.02900	0.02798	0.02699	0.02603	0.02509	28
29	0.03329	0.03213	0.03100	0.02990	0.02882	0.02778	0.02676	0.02578	0.02482	0.02389	29
30	0.03214	0.03098	0.02985	0.02875	0.02768	0.02664	0.02563	0.02465	0.02370	0.02278	30
31	0.03106	0.02990	0.02877	0.02768	0.02661	0.02557	0.02457	0.02360	0.02265	0.02174	31
32	0.03006	0.02889	0.02777	0.02667	0.02561	0.02458	0.02358	0.02261	0.02167	0.02077	32
33	0.02911	0.02795	0.02682	0.02573	0.02467	0.02364	0.02265	0.02169	0.02076	0.01986	33
34	0.02822	0.02706	0.02593	0.02484	0.02378	0.02276	0.02177	0.02082	0.01990	0.01901	34
35	0.02738	0.02622	0.02509	0.02400	0.02295	0.02193	0.02095	0.02000	0.01909	0.01821	35
36	0.02658	0.02542	0.02430	0.02321	0.02217	0.02115	0.02018	0.01923	0.01833	0.01745	36
37	0.02583	0.02467	0.02355	0.02247	0.02142	0.02041	0.01944	0.01851	0.01761	0.01674	37
38	0.02512	0.02396	0.02284	0.02176	0.02072	0.01972	0.01875	0.01782	0.01693	0.01607	38
39	0.02444	0.02329	0.02217	0.02109	0.02005	0.01905	0.01809	0.01717	0.01629	0.01544	39
40	0.02380	0.02265	0.02153	0.02046	0.01942	0.01843	0.01747	0.01656	0.01568	0.01484	40

ANNUAL SINKING FUND.

YRS.	0.25	0.50	0.75	1.00	RATE PER CENT. 1.25	1.50	1.75	2.00	2.25	2.50	YRS.
41	0.02319	0.02204	0.02092	0.01985	0.01882	0.01783	0.01688	0.01597	0.01510	0.01427	41
42	0.02261	0.02146	0.02034	0.01928	0.01825	0.01726	0.01632	0.01542	0.01455	0.01373	42
43	0.02206	0.02090	0.01979	0.01873	0.01770	0.01672	0.01579	0.01489	0.01403	0.01322	43
44	0.02153	0.02038	0.01927	0.01820	0.01719	0.01621	0.01528	0.01439	0.01354	0.01273	44
45	0.02102	0.01987	0.01877	0.01771	0.01669	0.01572	0.01479	0.01391	0.01307	0.01227	45
46	0.02054	0.01939	0.01828	0.01723	0.01622	0.01525	0.01433	0.01345	0.01262	0.01183	46
47	0.02008	0.01893	0.01783	0.01677	0.01576	0.01480	0.01389	0.01302	0.01219	0.01141	47
48	0.01963	0.01849	0.01739	0.01633	0.01533	0.01437	0.01347	0.01260	0.01178	0.01101	48
49	0.01921	0.01806	0.01696	0.01591	0.01492	0.01396	0.01306	0.01220	0.01139	0.01062	49
50	0.01880	0.01765	0.01656	0.01551	0.01452	0.01357	0.01267	0.01182	0.01102	0.01026	50
51	0.01841	0.01726	0.01617	0.01513	0.01414	0.01319	0.01230	0.01146	0.01066	0.00991	51
52	0.01803	0.01689	0.01580	0.01476	0.01377	0.01283	0.01195	0.01111	0.01032	0.00957	52
53	0.01767	0.01653	0.01544	0.01440	0.01342	0.01249	0.01160	0.01077	0.00999	0.00925	53
54	0.01732	0.01618	0.01509	0.01406	0.01308	0.01215	0.01128	0.01045	0.00968	0.00895	54
55	0.01698	0.01584	0.01476	0.01373	0.01275	0.01183	0.01096	0.01014	0.00937	0.00865	55
56	0.01666	0.01552	0.01443	0.01341	0.01244	0.01152	0.01066	0.00985	0.00909	0.00837	56
57	0.01635	0.01521	0.01412	0.01310	0.01213	0.01122	0.01037	0.00956	0.00881	0.00810	57
58	0.01604	0.01490	0.01383	0.01281	0.01184	0.01094	0.01009	0.00929	0.00854	0.00784	58
59	0.01575	0.01461	0.01354	0.01252	0.01156	0.01066	0.00981	0.00902	0.00828	0.00759	59
60	0.01547	0.01433	0.01326	0.01224	0.01129	0.01039	0.00955	0.00877	0.00804	0.00735	60

ANNUAL SINKING FUND.

YRS.	5.00	4.75	4.50	4.25	RATE PER CENT. 4.00	3.75	3.50	3.25	3.00	2.75	YRS.
1	1.00000	1.00000	1.00000	1.00000	1.00000	1.00000	1.00000	1.00000	1.00000	1.00000	1
2	0.48780	0.48840	0.48900	0.48960	0.49020	0.49080	0.49140	0.49200	0.49261	0.49322	2
3	0.31721	0.31799	0.31877	0.31956	0.32035	0.32114	0.32193	0.32273	0.32353	0.32433	3
4	0.23201	0.23288	0.23374	0.23462	0.23549	0.23637	0.23725	0.23814	0.23903	0.23992	4
5	0.18097	0.18188	0.18279	0.18371	0.18463	0.18555	0.18648	0.18742	0.18835	0.18930	5
6	0.14702	0.14795	0.14888	0.14982	0.15076	0.15171	0.15267	0.15363	0.15460	0.15557	6
7	0.12282	0.12376	0.12470	0.12565	0.12661	0.12757	0.12854	0.12952	0.13051	0.13150	7
8	0.10472	0.10566	0.10661	0.10756	0.10853	0.10950	0.11048	0.11146	0.11246	0.11346	8
9	0.09069	0.09163	0.09257	0.09353	0.09449	0.09547	0.09645	0.09744	0.09843	0.09944	9
10	0.07950	0.08044	0.08138	0.08233	0.08329	0.08426	0.08524	0.08623	0.08723	0.08824	10
11	0.07039	0.07131	0.07225	0.07319	0.07415	0.07512	0.07609	0.07708	0.07808	0.07909	11
12	0.06283	0.06374	0.06467	0.06560	0.06655	0.06751	0.06848	0.06947	0.07046	0.07147	12
13	0.05646	0.05736	0.05828	0.05920	0.06014	0.06110	0.06206	0.06304	0.06403	0.06503	13
14	0.05102	0.05192	0.05282	0.05374	0.05467	0.05561	0.05657	0.05754	0.05853	0.05952	14
15	0.04634	0.04722	0.04811	0.04902	0.04994	0.05088	0.05183	0.05279	0.05377	0.05476	15
16	0.04227	0.04314	0.04402	0.04491	0.04582	0.04674	0.04768	0.04864	0.04961	0.05060	16
17	0.03870	0.03955	0.04042	0.04130	0.04220	0.04311	0.04404	0.04499	0.04595	0.04693	17
18	0.03555	0.03638	0.03724	0.03811	0.03899	0.03990	0.04082	0.04175	0.04271	0.04368	18
19	0.03275	0.03357	0.03441	0.03526	0.03614	0.03703	0.03794	0.03887	0.03981	0.04078	19
20	0.03024	0.03105	0.03188	0.03272	0.03358	0.03446	0.03536	0.03628	0.03722	0.03817	20

ANNUAL SINKING FUND.

YRS.	2.75	3.00	3.25	3.50	RATE PER CENT. 3.75	4.00	4.25	4.50	4.75	5.00	YRS.
21	0.03582	0.03487	0.03394	0.03304	0.03215	0.03128	0.03043	0.02960	0.02879	0.02800	21
22	0.03369	0.03275	0.03183	0.03093	0.03006	0.02920	0.02836	0.02755	0.02675	0.02597	22
23	0.03174	0.03081	0.02991	0.02902	0.02815	0.02731	0.02649	0.02568	0.02490	0.02414	23
24	0.02997	0.02905	0.02815	0.02727	0.02642	0.02559	0.02478	0.02399	0.02322	0.02247	24
25	0.02834	0.02743	0.02654	0.02567	0.02483	0.02401	0.02321	0.02244	0.02169	0.02095	25
26	0.02684	0.02594	0.02506	0.02421	0.02337	0.02257	0.02178	0.02102	0.02028	0.01956	26
27	0.02546	0.02456	0.02370	0.02285	0.02203	0.02124	0.02047	0.01972	0.01899	0.01829	27
28	0.02418	0.02329	0.02244	0.02160	0.02080	0.02001	0.01925	0.01852	0.01781	0.01712	28
29	0.02299	0.02211	0.02127	0.02045	0.01965	0.01888	0.01813	0.01741	0.01672	0.01605	29
30	0.02188	0.02102	0.02018	0.01937	0.01859	0.01783	0.01710	0.01639	0.01571	0.01505	30
31	0.02085	0.02000	0.01917	0.01837	0.01760	0.01686	0.01614	0.01544	0.01478	0.01413	31
32	0.01989	0.01905	0.01823	0.01744	0.01668	0.01595	0.01524	0.01456	0.01391	0.01328	32
33	0.01899	0.01816	0.01735	0.01657	0.01582	0.01510	0.01441	0.01374	0.01310	0.01249	33
34	0.01815	0.01732	0.01653	0.01576	0.01502	0.01431	0.01363	0.01298	0.01236	0.01176	34
35	0.01736	0.01654	0.01575	0.01500	0.01427	0.01358	0.01291	0.01227	0.01166	0.01107	35
36	0.01661	0.01580	0.01503	0.01428	0.01357	0.01289	0.01223	0.01161	0.01101	0.01043	36
37	0.01591	0.01511	0.01435	0.01361	0.01291	0.01224	0.01160	0.01098	0.01040	0.00984	37
38	0.01525	0.01446	0.01370	0.01298	0.01229	0.01163	0.01100	0.01040	0.00983	0.00928	38
39	0.01462	0.01384	0.01310	0.01239	0.01171	0.01106	0.01044	0.00986	0.00930	0.00876	39
40	0.01403	0.01326	0.01253	0.01183	0.01116	0.01052	0.00992	0.00934	0.00880	0.00828	40

ANNUAL SINKING FUND.

RATE PER CENT.

YRS.	2.75	3.00	3.25	3.50	3.75	4.00	4.25	4.50	4.75	5.00	YRS.
41	0.01347	0.01271	0.01199	0.01130	0.01064	0.01002	0.00942	0.00885	0.00833	0.00782	41
42	0.01294	0.01219	0.01148	0.01080	0.01015	0.00954	0.00896	0.00841	0.00789	0.00739	42
43	0.01244	0.01170	0.01099	0.01033	0.00969	0.00909	0.00852	0.00798	0.00747	0.00699	43
44	0.01196	0.01123	0.01054	0.00988	0.00925	0.00866	0.00811	0.00758	0.00708	0.00662	44
45	0.01151	0.01079	0.01010	0.00945	0.00884	0.00826	0.00772	0.00720	0.00672	0.00626	45
46	0.01107	0.01036	0.00969	0.00905	0.00845	0.00788	0.00735	0.00684	0.00637	0.00593	46
47	0.01066	0.00996	0.00930	0.00867	0.00808	0.00752	0.00700	0.00651	0.00605	0.00561	47
48	0.01027	0.00958	0.00892	0.00831	0.00773	0.00718	0.00667	0.00619	0.00574	0.00532	48
49	0.00990	0.00921	0.00857	0.00796	0.00739	0.00686	0.00636	0.00589	0.00545	0.00504	49
50	0.00954	0.00887	0.00823	0.00763	0.00707	0.00655	0.00606	0.00560	0.00517	0.00478	50
51	0.00920	0.00853	0.00791	0.00732	0.00677	0.00626	0.00578	0.00533	0.00492	0.00453	51
52	0.00887	0.00822	0.00760	0.00702	0.00649	0.00598	0.00551	0.00508	0.00467	0.00429	52
53	0.00856	0.00791	0.00731	0.00674	0.00621	0.00572	0.00526	0.00483	0.00444	0.00407	53
54	0.00826	0.00763	0.00703	0.00647	0.00595	0.00547	0.00502	0.00461	0.00422	0.00386	54
55	0.00798	0.00735	0.00676	0.00621	0.00570	0.00523	0.00479	0.00439	0.00401	0.00367	55
56	0.00771	0.00708	0.00651	0.00597	0.00547	0.00500	0.00458	0.00418	0.00382	0.00348	56
57	0.00744	0.00683	0.00626	0.00573	0.00524	0.00479	0.00437	0.00399	0.00363	0.00330	57
58	0.00719	0.00659	0.00603	0.00551	0.00503	0.00458	0.00418	0.00380	0.00345	0.00314	58
59	0.00695	0.00636	0.00580	0.00529	0.00482	0.00439	0.00399	0.00362	0.00329	0.00298	59
60	0.00672	0.00613	0.00559	0.00509	0.00463	0.00420	0.00381	0.00345	0.00313	0.00283	60

ANNUAL SINKING FUND.

RATE PER CENT.

YRS.	5.25	5.50	5.75	6.00	6.25	6.50	6.75	7.00	7.25	7.50	YRS.
1	1.00000	1.00000	1.00000	1.00000	1.00000	1.00000	1.00000	1.00000	1.00000	1.00000	1
2	0.48721	0.48662	0.48603	0.48544	0.48485	0.48426	0.48368	0.48309	0.48251	0.48193	2
3	0.31643	0.31565	0.31488	0.31411	0.31334	0.31258	0.31181	0.31105	0.31029	0.30954	3
4	0.23115	0.23029	0.22944	0.22859	0.22775	0.22690	0.22606	0.22523	0.22440	0.22357	4
5	0.18007	0.17918	0.17828	0.17740	0.17651	0.17563	0.17476	0.17389	0.17303	0.17216	5
6	0.14610	0.14518	0.14427	0.14336	0.14246	0.14157	0.14068	0.13980	0.13892	0.13804	6
7	0.12189	0.12096	0.12005	0.11914	0.11823	0.11733	0.11644	0.11555	0.11467	0.11380	7
8	0.10379	0.10286	0.10195	0.10104	0.10013	0.09924	0.09835	0.09747	0.09659	0.09573	8
9	0.08976	0.08884	0.08793	0.08702	0.08613	0.08524	0.08436	0.08349	0.08262	0.08177	9
10	0.07858	0.07767	0.07676	0.07587	0.07498	0.07410	0.07324	0.07238	0.07153	0.07069	10
11	0.06947	0.06857	0.06768	0.06679	0.06592	0.06506	0.06420	0.06336	0.06252	0.06170	11
12	0.06192	0.06103	0.06015	0.05928	0.05842	0.05757	0.05673	0.05590	0.05508	0.05428	12
13	0.05556	0.05468	0.05382	0.05296	0.05212	0.05128	0.05046	0.04965	0.04885	0.04806	13
14	0.05015	0.04928	0.04843	0.04758	0.04676	0.04594	0.04514	0.04434	0.04357	0.04280	14
15	0.04548	0.04463	0.04379	0.04296	0.04215	0.04135	0.04057	0.03979	0.03903	0.03829	15
16	0.04142	0.04058	0.03976	0.03895	0.03816	0.03738	0.03661	0.03586	0.03512	0.03439	16
17	0.03786	0.03704	0.03624	0.03544	0.03467	0.03391	0.03316	0.03243	0.03171	0.03100	17
18	0.03473	0.03392	0.03313	0.03236	0.03160	0.03085	0.03013	0.02941	0.02871	0.02803	18
19	0.03194	0.03115	0.03038	0.02962	0.02888	0.02816	0.02745	0.02675	0.02607	0.02541	19
20	0.02945	0.02868	0.02792	0.02718	0.02646	0.02576	0.02507	0.02439	0.02373	0.02309	20

ANNUAL SINKING FUND.

YRS.	7.50	7.25	7.00	6.75	RATE PER CENT. 6.50	6.25	6.00	5.75	5.50	5.25	YRS.
21	0.02103	0.02165	0.02229	0.02294	0.02361	0.02430	0.02500	0.02573	0.02646	0.02722	21
22	0.01919	0.01979	0.02041	0.02104	0.02169	0.02236	0.02305	0.02375	0.02447	0.02521	22
23	0.01754	0.01812	0.01871	0.01933	0.01996	0.02061	0.02128	0.02196	0.02267	0.02339	23
24	0.01605	0.01661	0.01719	0.01778	0.01840	0.01903	0.01968	0.02035	0.02104	0.02174	24
25	0.01471	0.01525	0.01581	0.01639	0.01698	0.01759	0.01823	0.01888	0.01955	0.02024	25
26	0.01350	0.01402	0.01456	0.01512	0.01569	0.01629	0.01690	0.01754	0.01819	0.01887	26
27	0.01240	0.01290	0.01343	0.01396	0.01452	0.01510	0.01570	0.01631	0.01695	0.01761	27
28	0.01141	0.01189	0.01239	0.01291	0.01345	0.01401	0.01459	0.01519	0.01581	0.01646	28
29	0.01050	0.01096	0.01145	0.01195	0.01247	0.01302	0.01358	0.01416	0.01477	0.01540	29
30	0.00967	0.01012	0.01059	0.01107	0.01158	0.01210	0.01265	0.01322	0.01381	0.01442	30
31	0.00892	0.00935	0.00980	0.01027	0.01075	0.01126	0.01179	0.01234	0.01292	0.01351	31
32	0.00823	0.00864	0.00907	0.00952	0.01000	0.01049	0.01100	0.01154	0.01210	0.01268	32
33	0.00759	0.00799	0.00841	0.00884	0.00930	0.00978	0.01027	0.01079	0.01133	0.01190	33
34	0.00701	0.00740	0.00780	0.00822	0.00866	0.00912	0.00960	0.01010	0.01063	0.01118	34
35	0.00648	0.00685	0.00723	0.00764	0.00806	0.00851	0.00897	0.00946	0.00997	0.01051	35
36	0.00599	0.00635	0.00672	0.00710	0.00751	0.00794	0.00839	0.00887	0.00937	0.00989	36
37	0.00555	0.00588	0.00624	0.00661	0.00701	0.00742	0.00786	0.00832	0.00880	0.00931	37
38	0.00513	0.00545	0.00580	0.00615	0.00653	0.00694	0.00736	0.00780	0.00827	0.00877	38
39	0.00475	0.00506	0.00539	0.00573	0.00610	0.00649	0.00689	0.00733	0.00778	0.00826	39
40	0.00440	0.00470	0.00501	0.00534	0.00569	0.00607	0.00646	0.00688	0.00732	0.00779	40

ANNUAL SINKING FUND.

YRS.	5.25	5.50	5.75	6.00	6.25	6.50	6.75	7.00	7.25	7.50	YRS.
41	0.00734	0.00689	0.00646	0.00606	0.00568	0.00532	0.00498	0.00466	0.00436	0.00408	41
42	0.00693	0.00649	0.00607	0.00568	0.00532	0.00497	0.00464	0.00434	0.00405	0.00378	42
43	0.00654	0.00611	0.00571	0.00533	0.00498	0.00464	0.00433	0.00404	0.00376	0.00350	43
44	0.00618	0.00576	0.00537	0.00501	0.00466	0.00434	0.00404	0.00376	0.00349	0.00325	44
45	0.00583	0.00543	0.00505	0.00470	0.00437	0.00406	0.00377	0.00350	0.00325	0.00301	45
46	0.00551	0.00512	0.00476	0.00441	0.00410	0.00380	0.00352	0.00326	0.00302	0.00279	46
47	0.00521	0.00483	0.00448	0.00415	0.00384	0.00355	0.00329	0.00304	0.00281	0.00259	47
48	0.00493	0.00456	0.00422	0.00390	0.00360	0.00333	0.00307	0.00283	0.00261	0.00241	48
49	0.00466	0.00430	0.00397	0.00366	0.00338	0.00311	0.00287	0.00264	0.00243	0.00223	49
50	0.00441	0.00406	0.00374	0.00344	0.00317	0.00291	0.00268	0.00246	0.00226	0.00207	50
51	0.00417	0.00383	0.00353	0.00324	0.00297	0.00273	0.00250	0.00229	0.00210	0.00192	51
52	0.00395	0.00362	0.00332	0.00305	0.00279	0.00256	0.00234	0.00214	0.00196	0.00179	52
53	0.00373	0.00342	0.00313	0.00287	0.00262	0.00239	0.00219	0.00200	0.00182	0.00166	53
54	0.00354	0.00323	0.00295	0.00270	0.00246	0.00224	0.00204	0.00186	0.00169	0.00154	54
55	0.00335	0.00305	0.00278	0.00254	0.00231	0.00210	0.00191	0.00174	0.00158	0.00143	55
56	0.00317	0.00289	0.00263	0.00239	0.00217	0.00197	0.00179	0.00162	0.00147	0.00133	56
57	0.00300	0.00273	0.00248	0.00225	0.00204	0.00185	0.00167	0.00151	0.00137	0.00124	57
58	0.00285	0.00258	0.00234	0.00212	0.00191	0.00173	0.00156	0.00141	0.00127	0.00115	58
59	0.00270	0.00244	0.00221	0.00199	0.00180	0.00162	0.00146	0.00132	0.00119	0.00107	59
60	0.00256	0.00231	0.00208	0.00188	0.00169	0.00152	0.00137	0.00123			

RATE PER CENT.

ANNUAL SINKING FUND.

RATE PER CENT.

YRS.	10.00	9.75	9.50	9.25	9.00	8.75	8.50	8.25	8.00	7.75	YRS.
1	1.00000	1.00000	1.00000	1.00000	1.00000	1.00000	1.00000	1.00000	1.00000	1.00000	1
2	0.47619	0.47676	0.47733	0.47790	0.47847	0.47904	0.47962	0.48019	0.48077	0.48135	2
3	0.30211	0.30285	0.30358	0.30432	0.30505	0.30580	0.30654	0.30729	0.30803	0.30878	3
4	0.21547	0.21627	0.21706	0.21786	0.21867	0.21948	0.22029	0.22110	0.22192	0.22274	4
5	0.16380	0.16461	0.16544	0.16626	0.16709	0.16793	0.16877	0.16961	0.17046	0.17131	5
6	0.12961	0.13043	0.13125	0.13208	0.13292	0.13376	0.13461	0.13546	0.13632	0.13718	6
7	0.10541	0.10622	0.10704	0.10786	0.10869	0.10953	0.11037	0.11122	0.11207	0.11293	7
8	0.08744	0.08824	0.08905	0.08986	0.09067	0.09150	0.09233	0.09317	0.09401	0.09487	8
9	0.07364	0.07442	0.07520	0.07600	0.07680	0.07761	0.07842	0.07925	0.08008	0.08092	9
10	0.06275	0.06350	0.06427	0.06504	0.06582	0.06661	0.06741	0.06821	0.06903	0.06985	10
11	0.05396	0.05470	0.05544	0.05619	0.05695	0.05772	0.05849	0.05928	0.06008	0.06088	11
12	0.04676	0.04747	0.04819	0.04891	0.04965	0.05040	0.05115	0.05192	0.05270	0.05348	12
13	0.04078	0.04146	0.04215	0.04285	0.04357	0.04429	0.04502	0.04577	0.04652	0.04729	13
14	0.03575	0.03640	0.03707	0.03775	0.03843	0.03913	0.03984	0.04056	0.04130	0.04204	14
15	0.03147	0.03210	0.03274	0.03340	0.03406	0.03473	0.03542	0.03612	0.03683	0.03755	15
16	0.02782	0.02842	0.02903	0.02966	0.03030	0.03095	0.03161	0.03229	0.03298	0.03368	16
17	0.02466	0.02524	0.02583	0.02643	0.02705	0.02767	0.02831	0.02896	0.02963	0.03031	17
18	0.02193	0.02248	0.02305	0.02362	0.02421	0.02481	0.02543	0.02606	0.02670	0.02736	18
19	0.01955	0.02007	0.02061	0.02117	0.02173	0.02231	0.02290	0.02351	0.02413	0.02476	19
20	0.01746	0.01796	0.01848	0.01900	0.01955	0.02010	0.02067	0.02125	0.02185	0.02246	20

ANNUAL SINKING FUND.

RATE PER CENT.

YRS.	10.00	9.75	9.50	9.25	9.00	8.75	8.50	8.25	8.00	7.75	YRS.
21	0.01562	0.01610	0.01659	0.01710	0.01762	0.01815	0.01870	0.01926	0.01983	0.02042	21
22	0.01401	0.01446	0.01493	0.01541	0.01590	0.01641	0.01694	0.01748	0.01803	0.01860	22
23	0.01257	0.01300	0.01345	0.01391	0.01438	0.01487	0.01537	0.01589	0.01642	0.01697	23
24	0.01130	0.01171	0.01213	0.01257	0.01302	0.01349	0.01397	0.01447	0.01498	0.01551	24
25	0.01017	0.01056	0.01096	0.01138	0.01181	0.01225	0.01271	0.01319	0.01368	0.01419	25
26	0.00916	0.00953	0.00991	0.01031	0.01072	0.01114	0.01158	0.01204	0.01251	0.01299	26
27	0.00826	0.00861	0.00897	0.00934	0.00973	0.01014	0.01056	0.01100	0.01145	0.01192	27
28	0.00745	0.00778	0.00812	0.00848	0.00885	0.00924	0.00964	0.01006	0.01049	0.01094	28
29	0.00673	0.00704	0.00736	0.00770	0.00806	0.00842	0.00881	0.00920	0.00962	0.01005	29
30	0.00608	0.00637	0.00668	0.00700	0.00734	0.00769	0.00805	0.00843	0.00883	0.00924	30
31	0.00550	0.00577	0.00606	0.00637	0.00669	0.00702	0.00737	0.00773	0.00811	0.00850	31
32	0.00497	0.00523	0.00551	0.00579	0.00610	0.00641	0.00674	0.00709	0.00745	0.00783	32
33	0.00450	0.00475	0.00500	0.00528	0.00556	0.00586	0.00618	0.00651	0.00685	0.00721	33
34	0.00407	0.00431	0.00455	0.00481	0.00508	0.00536	0.00566	0.00597	0.00630	0.00665	34
35	0.00369	0.00391	0.00414	0.00438	0.00464	0.00491	0.00519	0.00549	0.00580	0.00613	35
36	0.00334	0.00355	0.00376	0.00399	0.00424	0.00449	0.00476	0.00504	0.00534	0.00566	36
37	0.00303	0.00322	0.00343	0.00364	0.00387	0.00411	0.00437	0.00464	0.00492	0.00523	37
38	0.00275	0.00293	0.00312	0.00332	0.00354	0.00377	0.00401	0.00427	0.00454	0.00483	38
39	0.00249	0.00266	0.00284	0.00303	0.00324	0.00345	0.00368	0.00393	0.00419	0.00446	39
40	0.00226	0.00242	0.00259	0.00277	0.00296	0.00316	0.00338	0.00361	0.00386	0.00412	40

YRS.	10.00	9.75	9.50	9.25	9.00	8.75	8.50	8.25	8.00	7.75	YRS.
41	0.00205	0.00220	0.00236	0.00253	0.00271	0.00290	0.00311	0.00333	0.00356	0.00381	41
42	0.00186	0.00200	0.00215	0.00231	0.00248	0.00266	0.00286	0.00306	0.00329	0.00352	42
43	0.00169	0.00182	0.00196	0.00211	0.00227	0.00244	0.00263	0.00282	0.00303	0.00326	43
44	0.00153	0.00165	0.00178	0.00193	0.00208	0.00224	0.00241	0.00260	0.00280	0.00302	44
45	0.00139	0.00150	0.00163	0.00176	0.00190	0.00205	0.00222	0.00240	0.00259	0.00279	45
46	0.00126	0.00137	0.00148	0.00161	0.00174	0.00189	0.00204	0.00221	0.00239	0.00258	46
47	0.00115	0.00125	0.00135	0.00147	0.00160	0.00173	0.00188	0.00204	0.00221	0.00239	47
48	0.00104	0.00113	0.00123	0.00134	0.00146	0.00159	0.00173	0.00188	0.00204	0.00222	48
49	0.00095	0.00103	0.00113	0.00123	0.00134	0.00146	0.00159	0.00173	0.00189	0.00205	49
50	0.00086	0.00094	0.00103	0.00112	0.00123	0.00134	0.00146	0.00160	0.00174	0.00190	50
51	0.00078	0.00086	0.00094	0.00103	0.00112	0.00123	0.00135	0.00147	0.00161	0.00176	51
52	0.00071	0.00078	0.00086	0.00094	0.00103	0.00113	0.00124	0.00136	0.00149	0.00163	52
53	0.00064	0.00071	0.00078	0.00086	0.00094	0.00104	0.00114	0.00125	0.00138	0.00151	53
54	0.00059	0.00065	0.00071	0.00079	0.00087	0.00095	0.00105	0.00116	0.00127	0.00140	54
55	0.00053	0.00059	0.00065	0.00072	0.00079	0.00088	0.00097	0.00107	0.00118	0.00130	55
56	0.00048	0.00054	0.00059	0.00066	0.00073	0.00081	0.00089	0.00099	0.00109	0.00120	56
57	0.00044	0.00049	0.00054	0.00060	0.00067	0.00074	0.00082	0.00091	0.00101	0.00112	57
58	0.00040	0.00044	0.00049	0.00055	0.00061	0.00068	0.00076	0.00084	0.00093	0.00103	58
59	0.00036	0.00040	0.00045	0.00050	0.00056	0.00062	0.00070	0.00077	0.00086	0.00096	59
60	0.00033	0.00037	0.00041	0.00046	0.00051	0.00057	0.00064	0.00072	0.00080	0.00089	60

RATE PER CENT.

Construction cost appraisal

AMOUNT OF POUND PER ANNUM.

YRS.	1	2	3	4	RATE PER CENT. 5	6	7	8	9	10	YRS.
1	1.000	1.000	1.000	1.000	1.000	1.000	1.000	1.000	1.000	1.000	1
2	2.010	2.020	2.030	2.040	2.050	2.060	2.070	2.080	2.090	2.100	2
3	3.030	3.060	3.091	3.122	3.152	3.184	3.215	3.246	3.278	3.310	3
4	4.060	4.122	4.184	4.246	4.310	4.375	4.440	4.506	4.573	4.641	4
5	5.101	5.204	5.309	5.416	5.526	5.637	5.751	5.867	5.985	6.105	5
6	6.152	6.308	6.468	6.633	6.802	6.975	7.153	7.336	7.523	7.716	6
7	7.214	7.434	7.662	7.898	8.142	8.394	8.654	8.923	9.200	9.487	7
8	8.286	8.583	8.892	9.214	9.549	9.897	10.260	10.637	11.028	11.436	8
9	9.369	9.755	10.159	10.583	11.027	11.491	11.978	12.488	13.021	13.579	9
10	10.462	10.950	11.464	12.006	12.578	13.181	13.816	14.487	15.193	15.937	10
11	11.567	12.169	12.808	13.486	14.207	14.972	15.784	16.645	17.560	18.531	11
12	12.683	13.412	14.192	15.026	15.917	16.870	17.888	18.977	20.141	21.384	12
13	13.809	14.680	15.618	16.627	17.713	18.882	20.141	21.495	22.953	24.523	13
14	14.947	15.974	17.086	18.292	19.599	21.015	22.550	24.215	26.019	27.975	14
15	16.097	17.293	18.599	20.024	21.579	23.276	25.129	27.152	29.361	31.772	15
16	17.258	18.639	20.157	21.825	23.657	25.673	27.888	30.324	33.003	35.950	16
17	18.430	20.012	21.762	23.698	25.840	28.213	30.840	33.750	36.974	40.545	17
18	19.615	21.412	23.414	25.645	28.132	30.906	33.999	37.450	41.301	45.599	18
19	20.811	22.841	25.117	27.671	30.539	33.760	37.379	41.446	46.018	51.159	19
20	22.019	24.297	26.870	29.778							

AMOUNT OF POUND PER ANNUM.

YRS.	1	2	3	4	5	6	7	8	9	10	YRS.
					RATE PER CENT.						
21	23.239	25.783	28.676	31.969	35.719	39.993	44.865	50.423	56.765	64.002	21
22	24.472	27.299	30.537	34.248	38.505	43.392	49.006	55.457	62.873	71.403	22
23	25.716	28.845	32.453	36.618	41.430	46.996	53.436	60.893	69.532	79.543	23
24	26.973	30.422	34.426	39.083	44.502	50.816	58.177	66.765	76.790	88.497	24
25	28.243	32.030	36.459	41.646	47.727	54.865	63.249	73.106	84.701	98.347	25
26	29.526	33.671	38.553	44.312	51.113	59.156	68.676	79.954	93.324	109.182	26
27	30.821	35.344	40.710	47.084	54.669	63.706	74.484	87.351	102.723	121.100	27
28	32.129	37.051	42.931	49.968	58.403	68.528	80.698	95.339	112.968	134.210	28
29	33.450	38.792	45.219	52.966	62.323	73.640	87.347	103.966	124.135	148.631	29
30	34.785	40.568	47.575	56.085	66.439	79.058	94.461	113.283	136.308	164.494	30
31	36.133	42.379	50.003	59.328	70.761	84.802	102.073	123.346	149.575	181.943	31
32	37.494	44.227	52.503	62.701	75.299	90.890	110.218	134.214	164.037	201.138	32
33	38.869	46.112	55.078	66.210	80.064	97.343	118.933	145.951	179.800	222.252	33
34	40.258	48.034	57.730	69.858	85.067	104.184	128.259	158.627	196.982	245.477	34
35	41.660	49.994	60.462	73.652	90.320	111.435	138.237	172.317	215.711	271.024	35
36	43.077	51.994	63.276	77.598	95.836	119.121	148.913	187.102	236.125	299.127	36
37	44.508	54.034	66.174	81.702	101.628	127.268	160.337	203.070	258.376	330.039	37
38	45.953	56.115	69.159	85.970	107.710	135.904	172.561	220.316	282.630	364.043	38
39	47.412	58.237	72.234	90.409	114.095	145.058	185.640	238.941	309.066	401.448	39
40	48.886	60.402	75.401	95.026	120.800	154.762	199.635	259.057	337.882	442.593	40

AMOUNT OF POUND PER ANNUM.

YRS.	11	12	13	14	RATE PER CENT. 15	16	17	18	19	20	YRS.
1	1.000	1.000	1.000	1.000	1.000	1.000	1.000	1.000	1.000	1.000	1
2	2.110	2.120	2.130	2.140	2.150	2.160	2.170	2.180	2.190	2.200	2
3	3.342	3.374	3.407	3.440	3.472	3.506	3.539	3.572	3.606	3.640	3
4	4.710	4.779	4.850	4.921	4.993	5.066	5.141	5.215	5.291	5.368	4
5	6.228	6.353	6.480	6.610	6.742	6.877	7.014	7.154	7.297	7.442	5
6	7.913	8.115	8.323	8.536	8.754	8.977	9.207	9.442	9.683	9.930	6
7	9.783	10.089	10.405	10.730	11.067	11.414	11.772	12.142	12.523	12.916	7
8	11.859	12.300	12.757	13.233	13.727	14.240	14.773	15.327	15.902	16.499	8
9	14.164	14.776	15.416	16.085	16.786	17.519	18.285	19.086	19.923	20.799	9
10	16.722	17.549	18.420	19.337	20.304	21.321	22.393	23.521	24.709	25.959	10
11	19.561	20.655	21.814	23.045	24.349	25.733	27.200	28.755	30.404	32.150	11
12	22.713	24.133	25.650	27.271	29.002	30.850	32.824	34.931	37.180	39.581	12
13	26.212	28.029	29.985	32.089	34.352	36.786	39.404	42.219	45.244	48.497	13
14	30.095	32.393	34.883	37.581	40.505	43.672	47.103	50.818	54.841	59.196	14
15	34.405	37.280	40.417	43.842	47.580	51.660	56.110	60.965	66.261	72.035	15
16	39.190	42.753	46.672	50.980	55.717	60.925	66.649	72.939	79.850	87.442	16
17	44.501	48.884	53.739	59.118	65.075	71.673	78.979	87.068	96.022	105.931	17
18	50.396	55.750	61.725	68.394	75.836	84.141	93.406	103.740	115.266	128.117	18
19	56.939	63.440	70.749	78.969	88.212	98.603	110.285	123.414	138.166	154.740	19
20	64.203	72.052	80.947	91.025	102.444	115.380	130.033	146.628	165.418	186.688	20

COMPOUND INTEREST. (AMOUNT OF POUND FACTORS.)

RATE PER CENT.

YRS.	1	2	3	4	5	6	7	8	9	10	YRS.
1	1.0100	1.0200	1.0300	1.0400	1.0500	1.0600	1.0700	1.0800	1.0900	1.1000	1
2	1.0201	1.0404	1.0609	1.0816	1.1025	1.1236	1.1449	1.1664	1.1881	1.2100	2
3	1.0303	1.0612	1.0927	1.1249	1.1576	1.1910	1.2250	1.2597	1.2950	1.3310	3
4	1.0406	1.0824	1.1255	1.1699	1.2155	1.2625	1.3108	1.3605	1.4116	1.4641	4
5	1.0510	1.1041	1.1593	1.2167	1.2763	1.3382	1.4026	1.4693	1.5386	1.6105	5
6	1.0615	1.1262	1.1941	1.2653	1.3401	1.4185	1.5007	1.5869	1.6771	1.7716	6
7	1.0721	1.1487	1.2299	1.3159	1.4071	1.5036	1.6058	1.7138	1.8280	1.9487	7
8	1.0829	1.1717	1.2668	1.3686	1.4775	1.5938	1.7182	1.8509	1.9926	2.1436	8
9	1.0937	1.1951	1.3048	1.4233	1.5513	1.6895	1.8385	1.9990	2.1719	2.3579	9
10	1.1046	1.2190	1.3439	1.4802	1.6289	1.7908	1.9672	2.1589	2.3674	2.5937	10
11	1.1157	1.2434	1.3842	1.5395	1.7103	1.8983	2.1049	2.3316	2.5804	2.8531	11
12	1.1268	1.2682	1.4258	1.6010	1.7959	2.0122	2.2522	2.5182	2.8127	3.1384	12
13	1.1381	1.2936	1.4685	1.6651	1.8856	2.1329	2.4098	2.7196	3.0658	3.4523	13
14	1.1495	1.3195	1.5126	1.7317	1.9799	2.2609	2.5785	2.9372	3.3417	3.7975	14
15	1.1610	1.3459	1.5580	1.8009	2.0789	2.3966	2.7590	3.1722	3.6425	4.1772	15
16	1.1726	1.3728	1.6047	1.8730	2.1829	2.5404	2.9522	3.4259	3.9703	4.5950	16
17	1.1843	1.4002	1.6528	1.9479	2.2920	2.6928	3.1588	3.7000	4.3276	5.0545	17
18	1.1961	1.4282	1.7024	2.0258	2.4066	2.8543	3.3799	3.9960	4.7171	5.5599	18
19	1.2081	1.4568	1.7535	2.1068	2.5270	3.0256	3.6165	4.3157	5.1417	6.1159	19
20	1.2202	1.4859	1.8061	2.1911	2.6533	3.2071	3.8697	4.6610	5.6044	6.7275	20

COMPOUND INTEREST. (AMOUNT OF POUND FACTORS.)

RATE PER CENT.

YRS.	1	2	3	4	5	6	7	8	9	10	YRS.
21	1.2324	1.5157	1.8603	2.2788	2.7860	3.3996	4.1406	5.0338	6.1088	7.4002	21
22	1.2447	1.5460	1.9161	2.3699	2.9253	3.6035	4.4304	5.4365	6.6586	8.1403	22
23	1.2572	1.5769	1.9736	2.4647	3.0715	3.8197	4.7405	5.8715	7.2579	8.9543	23
24	1.2697	1.6084	2.0328	2.5633	3.2251	4.0489	5.0724	6.3412	7.9111	9.8497	24
25	1.2824	1.6406	2.0938	2.6658	3.3864	4.2919	5.4274	6.8485	8.6231	10.8347	25
26	1.2953	1.6734	2.1566	2.7725	3.5557	4.5494	5.8074	7.3964	9.3992	11.9182	26
27	1.3082	1.7069	2.2213	2.8834	3.7335	4.8223	6.2139	7.9881	10.2451	13.1100	27
28	1.3213	1.7410	2.2879	2.9987	3.9201	5.1117	6.6488	8.6271	11.1671	14.4210	28
29	1.3345	1.7758	2.3566	3.1187	4.1161	5.4184	7.1143	9.3173	12.1722	15.8631	29
30	1.3478	1.8114	2.4273	3.2434	4.3219	5.7435	7.6123	10.0627	13.2677	17.4494	30
31	1.3613	1.8476	2.5001	3.3731	4.5380	6.0881	8.1451	10.8677	14.4618	19.1943	31
32	1.3749	1.8845	2.5751	3.5081	4.7649	6.4534	8.7153	11.7371	15.7633	21.1138	32
33	1.3887	1.9222	2.6523	3.6484	5.0032	6.8406	9.3253	12.6760	17.1620	23.2252	33
34	1.4026	1.9607	2.7319	3.7943	5.2533	7.2510	9.9781	13.6901	18.7284	25.5477	34
35	1.4166	1.9999	2.8139	3.9461	5.5160	7.6861	10.6766	14.7853	20.4140	29.1024	35
36	1.4308	2.0399	2.8983	4.1039	5.7918	8.1473	11.4239	15.9682	22.2512	30.9127	36
37	1.4451	2.0807	2.9852	4.2681	6.0814	8.6361	12.2236	17.2456	24.2538	34.0039	37
38	1.4595	2.1223	3.0748	4.4388	6.3855	9.1543	13.0793	18.6253	26.4367	37.4043	38
39	1.4741	2.1647	3.1670	4.6164	6.7048	9.7035	13.9948	20.1153	28.8160	41.1448	39
40	1.4889	2.2080	3.2620	4.8010	7.0400	10.2857	14.9745	21.7245	31.4094	45.2593	40

COMPOUND INTEREST. (AMOUNT OF POUND FACTORS.)

RATE PER CENT.

YRS.	1	2	3	4	5	6	7	8	9	10	YRS.
41	1.5038	2.2522	3.3599	4.9931	7.3920	10.9029	16.0227	23.4625	34.2363	49.7852	41
42	1.5188	2.2972	3.4607	5.1928	7.7616	11.5570	17.1443	25.3395	37.3175	54.7637	42
43	1.5340	2.3432	3.5645	5.4005	8.1497	12.2505	18.3444	27.3666	40.6761	60.2401	43
44	1.5493	2.3901	3.6715	5.6165	8.5572	12.9855	19.6285	29.5560	44.3370	66.2641	44
45	1.5648	2.4379	3.7816	5.8412	8.9850	13.7646	21.0025	31.9204	48.3273	72.8905	45
46	1.5805	2.4866	3.8950	6.0748	9.4343	14.5905	22.4726	34.4741	52.6767	80.1795	46
47	1.5963	2.5363	4.0119	6.3178	9.9060	15.4659	24.0457	37.2320	57.4176	88.1975	47
48	1.6122	2.5871	4.1323	6.5705	10.4013	16.3939	25.7289	40.2106	62.5852	97.0172	48
49	1.6283	2.6388	4.2562	6.8333	10.9213	17.3775	27.5299	43.4274	68.2179	106.7190	49
50	1.6446	2.6916	4.3839	7.1067	11.4674	18.4202	29.4570	46.9016	74.3575	117.3909	50
51	1.6611	2.7454	4.5154	7.3910	12.0408	19.5254	31.5190	50.6537	81.0497	129.1299	51
52	1.6777	2.8003	4.6509	7.6866	12.6428	20.6969	33.7253	54.7060	88.3442	142.0429	52
53	1.6945	2.8563	4.7904	7.9941	13.2749	21.9387	36.0861	59.0825	96.2951	156.2472	53
54	1.7114	2.9135	4.9341	8.3138	13.9387	23.2550	38.6121	63.8091	104.9617	171.8719	54
55	1.7285	2.9717	5.0821	8.6464	14.6356	24.6503	41.3150	68.9139	114.4083	189.0591	55
56	1.7458	3.0312	5.2346	8.9922	15.3674	26.1293	44.2070	74.4270	124.7050	207.9651	56
57	1.7633	3.0918	5.3917	9.3519	16.1358	27.6971	47.3015	80.3811	135.9285	228.7616	57
58	1.7809	3.1536	5.5534	9.7260	16.9426	29.3589	50.6127	86.8116	148.1620	251.6377	58
59	1.7987	3.2167	5.7200	10.1150	17.7897	31.1205	54.1555	93.7565	161.4966	276.8015	59
60	1.8167	3.2810	5.8916	10.5196	18.6792	32.9877	57.9464	101.2571	176.0313	304.4816	60

Construction cost appraisal

COMPOUND INTEREST. (AMOUNT OF POUND FACTORS.)

YRS.	11	12	13	14	15	16	17	18	19	20	YRS.
					RATE PER CENT.						
1	1.1100	1.1200	1.1300	1.1400	1.1500	1.1600	1.1700	1.1800	1.1900	1.2000	1
2	1.2321	1.2544	1.2769	1.2996	1.3225	1.3456	1.3689	1.3924	1.4161	1.4400	2
3	1.3676	1.4049	1.4429	1.4815	1.5209	1.5609	1.6016	1.6430	1.6852	1.7280	3
4	1.5181	1.5735	1.6305	1.6890	1.7490	1.8106	1.8739	1.9388	2.0053	2.0736	4
5	1.6851	1.7623	1.8424	1.9254	2.0114	2.1003	2.1924	2.2878	2.3864	2.4883	5
6	1.8704	1.9738	2.0820	2.1950	2.3131	2.4364	2.5652	2.6996	2.8398	2.9860	6
7	2.0762	2.2107	2.3526	2.5023	2.6600	2.8262	3.0012	3.1855	3.3793	3.5832	7
8	2.3045	2.4760	2.6584	2.8526	3.0590	3.2784	3.5115	3.7589	4.0214	4.2998	8
9	2.5580	2.7731	3.0040	3.2519	3.5179	3.8030	4.1084	4.4355	4.7854	5.1598	9
10	2.8394	3.1058	3.3946	3.7072	4.0456	4.4114	4.8068	5.2338	5.6947	6.1917	10
11	3.1518	3.4785	3.8359	4.2262	4.6524	5.1173	5.6240	6.1759	6.7767	7.4301	11
12	3.4985	3.8960	4.3345	4.8179	5.3503	5.9360	6.5801	7.2876	8.0642	8.9161	12
13	3.8833	4.3635	4.8980	5.4924	6.1528	6.8858	7.6987	8.5994	9.5964	10.6993	13
14	4.3104	4.8871	5.5348	6.2613	7.0757	7.9875	9.0075	10.1472	11.4198	12.8392	14
15	4.7846	5.4736	6.2543	7.1379	8.1371	9.2655	10.5387	11.9737	13.5895	15.4070	15
16	5.3109	6.1304	7.0673	8.1372	9.3576	10.7480	12.3303	14.1290	16.1715	18.4884	16
17	5.8951	6.8660	7.9861	9.2765	10.7613	12.4677	14.4265	16.6722	19.2441	22.1861	17
18	6.5436	7.6900	9.0243	10.5752	12.3755	14.4625	16.8790	19.6733	22.9005	26.6233	18
19	7.2633	8.6128	10.1974	12.0557	14.2318	16.7765	19.7484	23.2144	27.2516	31.9480	19
20	8.0623	9.6463	11.5231	13.7435	16.3665	19.4608	23.1056	27.3930	32.4294	38.3376	20

COMPOUND INTEREST. (AMOUNT OF POUND FACTORS.)

RATE PER CENT.

YRS.	11	12	13	14	15	16	17	18	19	20	YRS.
21	8.9492	10.8038	13.0211	15.6676	18.8215	22.5745	27.0336	32.3238	38.5910	46.0051	21
22	9.9336	12.1003	14.7138	17.8610	21.6447	26.1864	31.6293	38.1421	45.9233	55.2061	22
23	11.0263	13.5523	16.6266	20.3616	24.8915	30.3762	37.0062	45.0076	54.6487	66.2474	23
24	12.2392	15.1786	18.7881	23.2122	28.6252	35.2364	43.2973	53.1090	65.0320	79.4968	24
25	13.5855	17.0001	21.2305	26.4619	32.9190	40.8742	50.6578	62.6686	77.3881	95.3962	25
26	15.0799	19.0401	23.9905	30.1666	37.8568	47.4141	59.2697	73.9490	92.0918	114.4755	26
27	16.7386	21.3249	27.1093	34.3899	43.5353	55.0004	69.3455	87.2598	109.5892	137.3705	27
28	18.5799	23.8839	30.6335	39.2045	50.0656	63.8004	81.1342	102.9666	130.4112	164.8447	28
29	20.6237	26.7499	34.6158	44.6931	57.5755	74.0085	94.9271	121.5005	155.1893	197.8136	29
30	22.8923	29.9599	39.1159	50.9502	66.2118	85.8499	111.0646	143.3706	184.6753	237.3763	30
31	25.4104	33.5551	44.2010	58.0832	76.1435	99.5859	129.9456	169.1774	219.7636	284.8516	31
32	28.2056	37.5817	49.9471	66.2148	87.5651	115.5196	152.0364	199.6293	261.5187	341.8219	32
33	31.3082	42.0915	56.4402	75.4849	100.6998	134.0027	177.8826	235.5625	311.2073	410.1863	33
34	34.7521	47.1425	63.7774	86.0528	115.8048	155.4432	208.1226	277.9638	370.3366	492.2235	34
35	38.5749	52.7996	72.0685	98.1002	133.1755	180.3141	243.5035	327.9973	440.7006	590.6682	35
36	42.8181	59.1356	81.4374	111.8342	153.1518	209.1643	284.8991	387.0368	524.4337	708.8019	36
37	47.5281	66.2318	92.0243	127.4910	176.1246	242.6306	333.3319	456.7034	624.0761	850.5622	37
38	52.7562	74.1797	103.9874	145.3397	202.5433	281.4515	389.9983	538.9100	742.6506	1020.6747	38
39	58.5593	83.0812	117.5058	165.6873	232.9248	326.4837	456.2980	635.9138	883.7542	1224.8096	39
40	65.0009	93.0510	132.7816	188.8835	267.8635	378.7211	533.8687	750.3783	1051.6675	1469.7715	40

COMPOUND INTEREST. (AMOUNT OF POUND FACTORS.)

RATE PER CENT.

YRS.	21	22	23	24	25	26	27	28	29	30	YRS.
1	1.2100	1.2200	1.2300	1.2400	1.2500	1.2600	1.2700	1.2800	1.2900	1.3000	1
2	1.4641	1.4884	1.5129	1.5376	1.5625	1.5876	1.6129	1.6384	1.6641	1.6900	2
3	1.7716	1.8158	1.8609	1.9066	1.9531	2.0004	2.0484	2.0972	2.1467	2.1970	3
4	2.1436	2.2153	2.2889	2.3642	2.4414	2.5205	2.6014	2.6844	2.7692	2.8561	4
5	2.5937	2.7027	2.8153	2.9316	3.0518	3.1758	3.3038	3.4360	3.5723	3.7129	5
6	3.1384	3.2973	3.4628	3.6352	3.8147	4.0015	4.1959	4.3980	4.6083	4.8268	6
7	3.7975	4.0227	4.2593	4.5077	4.7684	5.0419	5.3288	5.6295	5.9447	6.2749	7
8	4.5950	4.9077	5.2389	5.5895	5.9605	6.3528	6.7675	7.2058	7.6686	8.1573	8
9	5.5599	5.9874	6.4439	6.9310	7.4506	8.0045	8.5948	9.2234	9.8925	10.6045	9
10	6.7275	7.3046	7.9259	8.5944	9.3132	10.0857	10.9153	11.8059	12.7614	13.7858	10
11	8.1403	8.9117	9.7489	10.6571	11.6415	12.7080	13.8625	15.1116	16.4622	17.9216	11
12	9.8497	10.8722	11.9912	13.2148	14.5519	16.0120	17.6053	19.3428	21.2362	23.2981	12
13	11.9182	13.2641	14.7491	16.3863	18.1899	20.1752	22.3588	24.7588	27.3947	30.2875	13
14	14.4210	16.1822	18.1414	20.3191	22.7374	25.4207	28.3957	31.6913	35.3391	39.3738	14
15	17.4494	19.7423	22.3140	25.1956	28.4217	32.0301	36.0625	40.5648	45.5875	51.1859	15
16	21.1138	24.0856	27.4462	31.2426	35.5271	40.3579	45.7994	51.9230	58.8079	66.5417	16
17	25.5477	29.3844	33.7588	38.7408	44.4089	50.8510	58.1652	66.4614	75.8621	86.5042	17
18	30.9127	35.8490	41.5233	48.0386	55.5112	64.0722	73.8698	85.0706	97.8622	112.4554	18
19	37.4043	43.7358	51.0737	59.5679	69.3889	80.7310	93.8147	108.8904	126.2422	146.1920	19
20	45.2593	53.3576	62.8206	73.8641	86.7362	101.7211	119.1446	139.3797	162.8524	190.0496	20

Index